Job Interview Questions and Answers

Guide to a Winning Interview with Amazing Interview Answers. Everything You Should Know to Be More Confident and Get the Job You Want.

Jim Hunting

Table of Contents

Introduction

Interview questions are designed to help the hiring manager understand you better as a person as well as whether you are qualified and can be successful in the role. Specifically, responses to questions are evaluated across many of the following categories (note that not all of these will apply to all roles):

- Do you have the education/training that is relevant to what this role requires? If not, can you demonstrate you can learn quickly and be effective? (What examples are provided to illustrate this?)
- Are you a team player, or more interested in personal credit and recognition? Will you work well with others? Do you help others even if "not part of your job description"?
- Are you mature? Do you get emotional or have unprofessional reactions to tough situations?
- Do you learn from past mistakes? I've never hired someone who couldn't provide a past mistake and what they learned from it.

- Will you fit in with the team? Will people respect you?
- Do you have critical thinking skills? Can you recognize what is important and not important in a given situation and not get bogged down in details?
- Do you communicate well both verbally and non-verbally? Are you concise, respectful, and able to provide the relevant information in any given situation?
- Can you manage conflict – whether with co-workers, managers, or subordinates?
- Do you put the interests of the company first?
- Are you a "go getter", or will you be a wallflower? I seldom am interested in hiring wallflowers.

Some other key items include never "bad mouthing" your previous boss, company, or co-workers. Always position conflict or reasons for leaving a company in a positive, educational light that made you a stronger person or reflected a change in career path.

One warning sign to watch out for: if a hiring manager asks you the same question, slightly rephrased, twice, then this is a sign you aren't providing the information needed from the question asked. Treat this as a WARNING. It means you need to stop and think a little more about the question and consider why the question is being asked relative to the categories outlined above, and then tailor your response to this.

To be honest, if I have to ask more than 3 or 4 questions over again because of poor responses, this is usually enough for me to terminate the interview, as my decision has already been made not to hire.

Conversely, if more than 2 or 3 responses are too lengthy, ramble and meander all over the place, I'm usually done with that candidate as well.

Remember – concise, relevant answers that don't have any personal, judgmental, or negative connotations in them.

Here are some great general questions to pick from to ask during the interview – *always* augment these with specific questions based on your research of the company and its products/services:

- What are the key challenges you see for this position?

- What are the priorities for the next 3 months for this role? What will success look like at that time?
- Is this a new role in the organization? If so, can you tell me more about the growth that resulted in the need for the role?
- What are the 3 top attributes or skills you think are needed to be successful in this role?
- What brought you to this company – e.g. what excites you about the company and the direction it is headed?
- How would you describe the culture of the company/group/etc.?
- What is your management style?

Chapter 1: Interview Selection Process

By the time you get to the interview, you are competing with people who are similarly qualified, perhaps in different ways. All the time I hear the complaint, "I can't believe they hired so and so when I'm so much more qualified!" Here's a reality check if you have ever felt that way. Technically speaking, you were *both* equally qualified to receive an interview. Your experience level may be different from his, even more than his, but his personality may make him the better match for the position.

When you're selected for an interview, you're in a group of several people a hiring manager decided could do the job. One person's experience or education level might be higher than another's. But after the paperwork was reviewed, the hiring manager determined you were all similarly qualified to be successful. Even if it looks as if someone received an interview because of his social networks, a hiring manager decided he could do the job.

There is a difference between meeting minimum qualifications and being similarly qualified. If you don't meet the minimum education or work qualifications listed on the job posting, your application generally won't even get a review. Similarly, qualified means that all applicants met the minimum qualifications. Thus, all are now eligible for further steps in the process. Now the selection process is about finding the one person who has the perfect mix of skills, personality and potential for success. You want to show the hiring manager that you are that one perfect match.

Beating the Competition

How does a hiring manager determine if someone has the perfect mix of skills to do a great job? Sometimes we get referrals. Sometimes we do a more thorough review of each resume or job application. Sometimes we conduct screening interviews with larger groups of applicants. But it all ends up at the same place: a final interview to see who gets the job. And at that point, how you present yourself is going to determine whether or not you get the job. Not your resume. Not your experience. Not your education. Not who referred you. At that point, it's all about the interview.

Once you're selected for that final interview, it becomes more about your interview performance than your minimum qualifications. You must prepare for that performance. It's partly about the chemistry between you and the interview team. It's also about how you represent the quality of your experience. At the interview, it's rarely about the actual years of experience.

You want *your* work history, whatever it is, to be judged the most applicable to the job. You want *your* answers to be the clearest. You want *your* personality to be likable without being obnoxious. Should you be yourself? Of course! Just be the most articulate, organized, and prepared version of yourself. That way, your experience, qualifications, and personality will shine through and wow the interview panel.

Chapter 2: What's the Best Way to Rehearse?

Most people will have access to, or can get access to, a video camera or a computer with built-in camera and microphone.

Rehearsing on your own is easily done, therefore, if you wish to do this before "showing off" with someone else.

If you decide to have some rehearsals on your own, be sure to act out as realistically as possible the interview situation.

Imagine that you are talking with an interviewer.

Most importantly, speak out - just thinking about it is better than doing no rehearsing, but speaking out your answers and questions is best.

Your mental rehearsals / visualization of your interview success is best done on your way into sleep when you are relaxed.

You should visualize your outstanding performance during the interview, if you wish, but, more importantly, visualize your celebrations after the interview process when you have received the job offer.

The purpose of rehearsal is to reduce your anxieties and fears and raise your performance standards.

Therefore, rehearse as many times as you feel you need and rehearse whatever you feel you need to (e.g. meeting the interviewer, interviews, leaving the interviewer).

Stay relaxed about your rehearsals though, don't get too intense about them.

In fact, have a bit of fun and laugh at your biggest mistakes.

In Summary:

* the best way to rehearse is to do a mock interview with a friend or 'mentor'

* mental rehearsal is also very helpful especially if you visualize success and celebration of it on your way into sleep when relaxed

* you can also rehearse on your own with a computer or video camera, but be sure to speak out.

Exercises to Do:

* test out the quality of your preparation by sharing it (or at least, the key points you have learned from it) with some trusted others, ask for some feedback, learn, do more preparation if necessary etc.

* in particular, prepare your lists of:

- questions you may be asked (arising from your C.V. / resume, and other questions, as illustrated above)

- difficult or awkward questions that you may encounter (from the examples above or from "gaps" in your C.V. / resume)

- questions you plan to ask if you get the opportunity

* practice your responses to the interview questions you have listed and record your efforts on your computer's audio / video system, or with a tape recorder / video camera etc.

* view the replays of your efforts (alone or with a 'mentor') and Analyze your performance both in terms of answers and in terms of your manner, presence, clarity, confidence and communications.

Capture in your learning log key opportunities to improve.

Repeat this exercise........

* enlist the help of a trusted friend to act as your interviewer and carry out a mock interview using the lists of questions you have prepared. Video tape this.

Seek positive feedback from your 'mentor' / video replay about the strengths and weaknesses of your performance.

Capture in your learning log what you should start doing, stop doing and do differently to improve your performance to "world champion level".

Repeat this exercise........

* on your way into sleep, visualize yourself in the interview situation performing as a true champion.

In particular, visualize the outcome of your interviews when you receive the job offer.

Imagine your family and friends and colleagues congratulating you and everyone, especially you, smiling and laughing and celebrating your great success.

Make this as vivid and real as you can in your mind.

Imagine the colours and sounds. Feel the positive happy emotions that you would feel.

Chapter 3: Background and Personality Questions

What are some characteristics of a successful team?

Question Type:

Background and Personality

Question Analysis:

The interviewer will typically associate the team characteristics in in your response with your own personal working habits and gauge whether you are a good fit within their team. Your answer should focus on characteristics that align well with the company's values and are part of successful team dynamics. Some common characteristics of successful teams to consider are: effective communication, strong collaboration, diverse backgrounds and skillsets, goal driven, strong leadership, supportive, and ability to execute.

What to Avoid:

Even though it is common for teams to joke around and partake in social activities, your answer should avoid unprofessional characteristics such as "knows how to relax and have fun" or "likes to joke around."

Example Response:

Successful teams are made up of people who know how to work together to achieve a common goal. They are centered around strong leadership, effective communication and collaboration, and diverse backgrounds and skillsets. They are also goal driven and know how to complete a task.

Are you willing to work overtime or on weekends if necessary?

Question Type:

Background and Personality

Question Analysis:

Even if there will be very little need to work overtime or on weekends, the interviewer will often use this question to determine the candidate's willingness to be flexible to meet the company's needs. If the company only asks an employee to work odd hours once a year for a one-off project, they want to know that the employee prioritizes their job and has a "whatever it takes" attitude to get it done. Your answer should show your willingness to work when needed but also be honest if you have limitations on your flexibility.

What to Avoid:

You should avoid going into too many unnecessary details about your personal life or commitments. You should also not commit to something if it is not feasible. Be sure to show your willingness to go above and beyond when necessary but also be open about limitations.

Example Response:

I have two young children who are involved in sports and after school activities. For a couple of their teams, I help out as an assistant coach. With that said, I am willing and able to work outside of normal hours when needed. I can be most flexible when I am notified in advance so I am able to arrange my schedule.

Tell me about a time you went out of your way to strengthen a client, customer, or team member relationship.

Question Type:

Behavioral

Question Analysis:

Cultivating strong working relationships requires much more than a technical skillset. The interviewer will get a good sense of the candidate's interpersonal communication skills throughout the interview process, but they will use this question to find out if the candidate only focuses on their own work and objectives or if they are willing to take the time and energy to invest in internal and external working relationships. You should discuss an example that demonstrates strong soft skills and shows your willingness to go above and beyond for a co-worker or client.

What to Avoid:

You should avoid examples that would be expected under normal circumstances such as "When any of our clients send me an email, I always make sure to respond within 24 hours." You should also stay clear of examples that are not professional. "I take a new co-worker out for lunch at least once a month" is okay but it is best to avoid, "I take my team to the bar when we beat our sales numbers."

Example Response:

S: In my previous role as a digital advertising sales representative, I led a team working on a new client project to produce twenty-five digital ads for a social media campaign. We kept our client contact updated on our work at each project milestone. As we approached the wrap up stages of the project, she surprised all of us by changing her mind and asking us to adjust the background colors and design of each ad.

T: Our team was frustrated because we had received positive affirmation on the ads until the very end of the project. We estimated that the edits would take an additional ten hours of work and initially considered asking the client for further payment on top of the initial project fee.

A: Before expressing our frustration and asking for further payment, I set up a meeting with our contact to better understand the situation. Instead of leading the conversation with our frustration, I asked about the changes and found out that it was actually her boss who changed his mind about the ads. She apologized and sympathized with the difficult situation it put us in. I told her I understood that these things happen and agreed to make the edits at no additional charge. We put in the extra work to deliver the project on time and I brought in bagels and coffee for the client and her team at the closing meeting.

R: Our contact was very appreciative of our hard work and willingness to go above and beyond to meet their needs. They had excellent results from the advertisements and ended up hiring us for three additional projects over the next year.

Tell me about a time you did not meet a goal. What did you learn?

Question Type:

Behavioral

Question Analysis:

Like the "describe a failure" question #19, you should not feel uncomfortable discussing a time you did not achieve a goal. As long as you continue to set challenging goals, you will come up short from time to time and the interviewer knows this. The key is to be able to explain to the interviewer why you did not meet the goal and show them that you learned from it.

What to Avoid:

You should avoid placing blame on a co-worker or outside circumstances. The interviewer is looking for an example in which you take responsibility for coming up short. With that said, you should be careful not to provide an example where you failed as a result of negligence or a poor work ethic.

Example Response:

S/T: In my prior role as a business analyst, my manager asked me to create a step-by-step visual tutorial on how to run ten different financial reports in our ERP system. She mentioned that the tutorials were urgently needed for a department project and asked me to estimate how long it would take to have it completed.

A: After reviewing the first couple reports I mentioned to her that I could finish all of the tutorials within two days. Shortly after, I realized I had not reviewed my calendar before making the commitment and I had four important meetings over the next two days which could not be rescheduled. To make matters worse, it quickly became evident that my estimate of time needed to complete the project was too optimistic.

R: I worked thirteen-hour days to try to meet the goal, but it ended up taking me four days to complete the tutorials instead of two. I took full responsibility for the delay when explaining to my manager that I had failed to consider my other obligations and did a poor job of estimating the number of hours the project would require. When setting deadlines for my work, I have learned to take the time to create a comprehensive plan that incorporates all factors and obligations. I have also learned that it is great to set challenging goals, but they should always be realistic and attainable.

How long would you plan to stay with the company?

Question Type:

Ambition

Question Analysis:

Employees are not as loyal to their employers as in the past. Hiring can be a risky investment if a candidate is likely to bounce around to other companies whenever new opportunities arise. The interviewer is looking for the candidate to convince them that they are committed to the position. Your answer should focus on your enthusiasm for the opportunities within the company and position and your desire to remain with the company as long as you are continuing to grow and have a positive impact.

If you do have plans to leave town within a couple of years due to a certain circumstance (such as having a spouse in the military), be honest and upfront about it with the interviewer but if there are opportunities to work remotely, leave the door open to continue with the company.

What to Avoid:

Your answer should avoid contingencies based on promotions or pay increases such as "I'll continue to work here as long as I am paid fairly." You have not established credibility with the employer so an answer like this answer can be off-putting to the interviewer.

Example Response:

I am excited about this position but even more so about the career opportunities working for XYZ Company. The rotational program in the marketing department enables new employees to obtain experience working in many diverse roles over their first three years with the company. I think this program would enhance my skillset and position me for future leadership roles. As long as I continue to bring value and make positive contributions, I would plan on remaining with the company.

If an urgent work situation came up over the weekend, how would you react?

Question Type:

Background and Personality

Question Analysis:

This can be a tricky question for some candidates because they interpret it as the interviewer asking if they will always be "on call." However, this is usually not the objective of the question. Instead, the interviewer wants to know that if a rare and urgent situation arose outside of normal work hours, the candidate would be willing to do whatever they could to help remediate it. You should demonstrate your willingness to help out if an urgent situation came up outside of normal work hours.

What to Avoid:

There is nothing wrong with emphasizing your belief in a work-life balance, but you should never say anything to indicate that you completely ignore work outside of the office such as "I turn my work phone off when I leave the office" or "I ignore all work communication on the weekends." On the other end of the spectrum, your answer should also not be "I make myself available at all times." The interviewer knows this is not possible.

Example Response:

I strongly believe in the benefits of finding a good work-life balance. However, the timing of urgent issues can be unpredictable. If something came up outside of work hours that required immediate attention, I would do whatever I could to help fix the problem.

What are some ways you deal with an upset customer or client?

Question Type:

Background and Personality

Question Analysis:

Individual interactions with vendors, clients, and customers can be reflective of the whole company. The interviewer wants to know that the candidate will be a good representative of the company, especially under pressure and difficult situations. Your answer should show that you know how to remain calm, respectful, and avoid being combative when dealing with an upset customer.

What to Avoid:

You should avoid only discussing how you **talk** to upset customers. Usually, the most important thing to do in this situation is to show the customer you are willing to **listen** to their frustration and sympathize with them. You should also avoid generic canned responses such as "my philosophy is that the customer is always right."

Example Response:

Before I try to offer any type of response or resolution, I first like to show the customer that I am willing to listen to their issue. Typically, the most effective way to calm the situation is to simply take the time to hear the customer and show sympathy for their frustration. When speaking with the customer, I am always mindful of my tone and body language to ensure I do not come across as combative. I try to come to a fair resolution and help the customer in any way I can within the company's policies. If I am not able to come to a resolution or need to look further into the problem, I take down their contact information and follow back up with them as soon as possible.

How do you ensure quality in your work?

Question Type:

Background and Personality

Question Analysis:

The interviewer will use this question to determine how important quality is to the candidate. They are looking for the candidate to discuss procedures they implement to ensure that their work is rooted in quality. You should emphasize your desire for quality work and discuss a process you use to ensure mistakes are limited.

What to Avoid:

The interviewer knows everyone makes mistakes, so you should avoid answers such as "I make almost no mistakes in my work." You also want to stay away from placing the burden on others with a response such as "I usually ask someone else to review my work." The interviewer is looking for you to discuss your own process to mitigate mistakes before it gets reviewed or submitted.

Example Response:

I consider myself to be an efficient worker, but I also take the time to pay close attention to detail in my work. Before I start any task, I step back to ensure I understand the full scope of the work and consider all factors. If there are questions around the deliverables, I make sure to find the answer or reach out to someone who can clarify for me. I would rather get it right the first time than have to go back and redo work. After completing my work, I always go back through it and do a detailed self-review to ensure accuracy and quality. Although I still make the occasional mistake, my process has worked well in maintaining high quality and limiting mistakes before my work gets submitted to someone else.

Are you willing to travel for this job?

Question Type:

Background and Personality

Question Analysis:

The interviewer will typically ask this question only when the job does require some level of travel. They are looking to confirm that the candidate has read the job description (which should indicate the amount of travel) and is agreeable with the travel requirements. Your answer should affirm that you are comfortable with the travel requirements in the job description. If the job description did not mention travel, then you should be upfront and honest about your ability to travel. Be sure to state any travel limitations during the week (such as only able to travel Mon-Fri). If you would like to learn more specifics about the travel requirements, you can find out more with a follow up question at the end of your response.

What to Avoid:

You should never tell the interviewer you are not willing to travel any less than what is stated in the job description. For example, if the description says out-of-town travel is required up to 50% of the time, you should not have applied to the job if you are only willing to travel occasionally. If you are flexible and willing to travel whenever needed, you can let the interviewer know. You should avoid discussing ulterior motives for traveling such as "I never miss a chance to get out of town for a free hotel room and free food" or "I have over 100,000 Marriott points, I would love to get more."

Example Response:

I worked as an account executive in the past and was on the road about 40% of the time. The travel did not bother me at all. When I reviewed the description for this position, it had indicated that travel would be required up to 20% of the time. However, I am flexible to travel beyond that if needed. Would the travel be during certain times of the year or more sporadic?

Tell me about a time you dealt with conflicting priorities. How did you determine the top priority?

Question Type:

Behavioral

Question Analysis:

The interviewer will ask this question to assess the candidate's organizational and decision-making skills. Situations will often come up requiring you to organize your time to manage multiple tasks and effectively prioritize them. Your answer should demonstrate your ability to choose the top priority while not neglecting your responsibilities for the secondary priorities.

What to Avoid:

Prioritizing multiple tasks is much different than "multitasking" which infers that you work on multiple tasks at the same time. You should avoid stating that you like to multitask. Most studies show that multitasking hurts focus, sacrifices quality, and leads to less efficiency.

Example Response:

S: In my previous position selling CRM software, my manager had signed our team up for an out-of-town two-day training event. Three hours before my flight was to depart, the contact at my largest account in the area called me frantically explaining that their software had crashed.

T: My manager was already on a prior flight, so I was unable to get ahold of her at the time. After considering the circumstances, I decided that the best course of action was to drive directly to the client's office to help them resolve the urgent problem.

A: I spent the next four hours working with the client and our IT department until the issue was resolved. I then called my manager and explained why I missed my flight and let her know that the client was very appreciative that I had made myself available right away.

R: My manager told me I made the right decision and said it could have been disastrous if our client had to wait longer to get the assistance they needed. I booked a later flight that evening and made it to the training on time.

Chapter 4: Questions to Understand Your Personality

The employer knows who you are as a person, but they will want to really understand what it's like to spend time with you. How will you fit in with the rest of the team? What will it be like when you have to make a decision? Can you actually lead or are you just saying that?

These are more complex questions to dig deeper into your personality. Anyone can come up with the perfect response to the previous questions we discussed, but these are prompts that force you to be honest about who you are. There is no faking when it comes to crafting these responses!

"Tell me about a time you had to apologize to a friend or family member, and how you were able to rectify the situation."

This can be a pretty tricky one to answer, but there are times that it has been asked in an interview. The point is not to shame you or call you out. What they are looking for is your ability to take accountability. Can you admit when you are wrong? Can you acknowledge other people? Do you understand the various perspectives around a situation? Of course, don't share the most dramatic fight you've ever had, but don't be afraid to be honest! Let them really know what happened and show that you can take responsibility for things. Here's what you might say:

"There was one time when I was on a trip with my Mom and sister. My Mom believed that we should go south to get to a restaurant, and I thought we had to go north. She insisted she checked, but I believed that I was right based on what I remembered from before. Turns out, she was right. I apologized and learned that I should always double check before I assume that I'm certain. Not only did I make myself look silly, but I invalidated my mother's intelligence."

"What would your ultimate dream job be?"

Your dream job might be to lay on the beach and have people pay you to do nothing all day but eat delicious snacks. You can say this if you want, but they will really be wanting to know what type of personality you have. Be truthful and apply it to the job while also refrain from obviously schmoozing them. You might say something like this:

"My dream position would be one where I can have creative freedom while also having a team around me that can help support me with my accountability deadlines, or someone that offers creative perspectives when I'm stuck. I would want a changing environment where I could grow, but one that is also reliable that I know I will have around because job security is important to me."

"How do you motivate yourself when you feel like you don't want to do anything?"

Motivation is a key factor in many positions. The person conducting the interview will simply want to know how you are able to motivate yourself even when you feel like you want to do nothing at all. This is a potential answer that you could share if asked:

"Motivation is best when it comes from within myself. I'll usually try to reward myself. Maybe if I get a project done early then I'll go out for lunch rather than eating what I already packed. If I can't find that motivation within myself, then I like talking to friends and family who encourage me to keep going, or I might listen to some of my favorite songs or read cheesy quotes that help to inspire me!"

"What app on your phone do you use most at the moment?"

This is to get a sense of the type of person that you are. Is it a phone game that you spend most of your time on? Are you someone who is always reading the news? This is just a fun question that will help you to showcase a little bit more about your personality. Be honest! Don't make something up just to sound smarter, because it could be the same app the person conducting the interview uses, and they might want to start a conversation about it that you won't be able to honestly participate in. You might consider saying something like this:

"The app that I probably use the most would be a split between Photos and Instagram. I love taking photographs, editing them, and having memories stored in my phone of my closest loved ones. I also love looking at pictures, keeping up with the news, and chatting with online friends, which I can do through Instagram."

"If you could change one thing about your appearance, what would it be? If you could change something about your personality, what would it be?"

This is a tricky question that might throw you off, but it's also a fun one that gives the person conducting the interview an idea of how you think. What is it that you think is the most important thing to change about your physical appearance? What about your personality? It's going to be important that you are self-aware and understanding of what issues you might need to improve on. You also don't want to be too harsh on yourself. Here is a good answer that you might want to include:

"If I could change one thing about my appearance, I would probably want to whiten my teeth! I think a bright smile is important for spreading positivity and showing that I'm friendly. For my personality, I would also want to be less critical and nicer to myself so that I have more confidence."

"Can you describe a time when you really "learned your lesson," or had an enlightening moment that you still frequently apply to your current life?"

The person conducting the interview is not going to expect that you are perfect. What they will be the most concerned about is that even if you do have a flaw, you know exactly what you need to do to fix it. They want to know that whatever issues you might have, you have the ability to recognize what needs to be learned from the situation and that you had learned the lesson. Life is not about regretting your mistakes, it's about learning from them. Here's what you might say:

"There was one time when I found myself very stressed out from work on Friday to the point that I couldn't enjoy my weekend because I had so much to do on Monday. I had a fun trip planned that was completely ruined by my anxiety over work on Monday. I learned that it was most important for me to get my work done on time so that I could enjoy my time off work more."

"How do you normally interact with coworkers?"

Some environments will be completely isolated, and you won't have to talk to a soul. Others will require complete collaboration. This is a good question to help the person asking to know whether or not you will be able to work well with the rest of the team. Be honest, if you have friends from previous positions, that's great! If you struggled to mingle, share why.

"I can be shy at first, sometimes afraid to let others get to know me, but once I've found my footing and become comfortable, it's easy for me to open up and make friends. Getting along with others is important to me so that I can enjoy my work that much more, and it makes the job a lot more fun as well."

"What is a superficial fear, something not related to being alone or failing?"

This question is one that will be specifically targeted at figuring out what your fears on a deeper level might be. are you afraid of spiders? Clowns? The dark? All of these are perfectly fine! They just want to get to know your personality and want you to avoid the common answer - that you are afraid of failing, because this is what most will answer with. Here is an example of what you might actually want to say:

"I'm pretty afraid of the dark! I don't like when it's pitch black, so I usually keep a night light around. Other than that, I don't have big fears that keep me from working! I actually enjoy situations that might be a little more thrilling, like scary movies or roller coasters."

"Can you describe yourself in three words or less?"

This is a common question that will likely be asked frequently, but it's also a hard one that you might struggle to come up with answers to! Don't overthink it. Think about keywords that might have been in the job description which can help you better determine what they might be looking for. Include a professional trait, a real authentic trait, and one that is related to your personality – who you really are deep down. Rather than give you an exact answer, here are some keywords that you likely have, but will also help to make you sound great:

Reliable

Trustworthy

Funny

Logical

Positive

Practical

Realistic

Dependable

Brave

Proud

Virtuous

Witty

Artistic

Educated

Flexible

"What did you enjoy most about elementary school? High school? College? Post-grad?"

They've already learned about who you are and what your background is, but they still want to get to know who you really are. We all have experiences that helped to identify us, but it is our emotions, feelings, and reactions that really help to make up the person that we are. They will likely ask what you liked most about school, so be honest!

"When I was in school, I used to love science classes. I was always curious about the way the world worked. As I made my way into high school, I focused more on arts and expressing myself. When I entered college, I started to really be more interested in the community that surrounded me and how I could actually affect the people in the community."

"What do you remember most about your childhood?"

When you are asked to reflect back and look on your childhood, you will want to focus on positive and happy memories. Sadly, some of us have been through more challenging situations in our lives that we wish to not remember, but now is not the time to share them. Instead, bring up something that you remember that has become a part of your character, even if it was challenging.

"I remember always being interested in learning more and finding out as much new information as I possibly could. I also remember having a single mother who worked two jobs. This curiosity of the world along with the hard work that my mother exemplified helped me to become the dedicated person that I am today. Even when things were more challenging, my Mom had a positive attitude and that has stuck with me to this day."

"Let's say you are in a position where you have been given several tasks to complete by a certain deadline. You realize that even if you worked non-stop as hard as you could, it's still an unrealistic deadline. How would you handle this situation?"

This is a common thing that you might run into in real life. Sometimes we have a ton of work to do, and we want to do it, but we just don't have the time to actually complete the tasks reasonably. Even if we try as hard as we can, there is still always the chance that we might exhaust ourselves in the process. Your employer doesn't want to hear that "this wouldn't be a problem for me," because that's unrealistic. Answer honestly! Say something like this:

"I would start by making a list of what I had to do and prioritize things that are the most important. I would make sure that I am taking care of those first. After working for a little bit and getting a better sense of what I can and cannot realistically complete, that is when I would consider talking to my supervisor. I would express to them what my issue was, and what I would need from them. I would still focus on getting as much work done as possible because making incremental progress is better than doing nothing at all."

"Are you more concerned with the overall big picture, or do you care about every tiny detail?"

Many people will categorize themselves as someone that either looks at the overall idea of something, or the type of person that hangs onto every last detail. For most of the questions we've gone over already and others that we'll be touching on, remember that you don't always have to be one or the other. You could find a way to describe yourself as someone in the middle.

"I think this is situational for me. I usually create a plan based around the small details with the bigger goal in mind. As I work, I pay attention to as much as I can. However, I check in with myself and make sure that I remember the big picture. If I don't, it becomes easy to hang onto the very smallest issues, which could waste time."

"What did you want to be when you "grew up"?"

This is a question that will be directly related to your personality. It is something that will help them discover if this position is something that you have wanted all of your life, or if you have only recently become interested in this field. Be honest, and don't try and pretend that you've wanted to be an accountant since you were five years old. If you did, all the more power to you! However, your interviewer will likely know that you are being inauthentic if you make up a lie just to look better in this situation.

"When I was little, I always wanted to be a teacher and a dancer. I love dancing and expressing myself, but I also admired the many teachers that I had growing up. Since then I've outgrown these dreams, but I still have that same passion and compassion that I admired as a child."

"If you had to pick a career completely unrelated to this field, what would it be?"

This is a fun question that many employers will want to hear from you. If you weren't doing what you are doing, what would you be doing in a nutshell? If you are working a retail job to help you get through college while you are studying to become a nurse, then you would probably tell them that you want to be a nurse since that's your eventual goal. However, take this opportunity to be creative if you want and share what you would consider completely unrelated to anything that you are a part of. Here's what you might say:

"Being a financial advisor is what I want to do now, but I always had dreams of being a veterinarian. I would have considered this field, but blood and surgery makes me queasy so I don't think I would have lasted long! I still love animals, but I understand now that my true talents lie within this field."

Chapter 5: Questions about your former workplace.

How do you fit in with a new company's culture?

Every company has its own unique culture and it always takes some getting used to when you change jobs. There may even be some nuances of different cultures between departments. The interviewer wants to know that you'll go with the flow –not expect the culture to change to your standards, but that you'll adapt to the company's culture. I find just talking with people helps clarify and solidify expectations for behavior and norms. I'm pretty good at reading people, but if I make a misstep, I apologize immediately and profusely. Then I change whatever I did wrong so that I'm conforming to the company's norms. There's usually at least one friendly person who'll help a new person navigate their way through the company's culture and I've always been fortunate to be able to find such people.

How have you personally impacted employee safety?

Safety is everyone's business, and if everyone's not watching out for everyone else, accidents can happen.

I strongly believe it's each of our jobs to ensure employee safety, and to look out for one another, stopping or preventing accidents from happening. Just a few weeks ago, I was walking through the shop and I noticed that an employee was preparing to pour a clear liquid into a 55-gallon drum that was labeled 'Acetone'. The container the employee was pouring from wasn't marked with the contents, so I asked her. She said it was Alcohol. I pointed out that the barrel into which she planned to pour the Alcohol was labeled Acetone, and it probably wasn't a good idea to mix two chemicals.

We laughed about it, but it could have been serious. She and I then went to her supervisor together and suggested that all the 'interim' containers for used chemicals be labeled for specific chemicals only. BONUS POINTS: The other employee and I made it our project to make labels for all the interim containers and show all the employees what we'd done so two chemicals didn't accidentally get mixed.

Tell me something you would have done differently at work, if you could have a 'Do-Over'.

The employer is checking to make sure you understand the importance of Continuous Improvement and the only way to do that is to constantly be on the look-out for newer, better, faster, cheaper ways of doing things. If you simply imply the identification of improvements is someone else's job, it won't look particularly favorable for you. **This is another area that is everyone's responsibility. If we see something that could easily be tweaked to improve the way it works, we should suggest it or just tackle it ourselves.**

What can you do better for us than our other candidates for the job? The employer wants you to identify your strengths for them. I'm sure your other candidates have their own strengths, but I do know that one of my strengths is not to accept the status quo. If I recognize a better way of doing something, I'll speak up, or if it's part of my own job, I'll just change the process. It makes no sense to just keep doing something the same way it's always been done, just because it's always been done that way.

I think another differentiator for me is my Positive Attitude. Rather than seeing the worst in a person or situation, I look for the good. There's good to be had in everyone and everything, and we're all here for the same reason. I work hard to build on the good, making sure my own work is top-notch and others' work is the very best it can be.

Have you ever had difficulty working with any manager?

Employers will want to know whether you have problems taking direction from ANY manager, not just those younger than yourself. Are you the type that can't stand to have anyone tell you how to do something? Like to figure things out for yourself? Then start your own business. Otherwise, learn how to take direction gracefully and gratefully from others. Not at all. I'll take direction from anyone who knows more than I do – and that's everyone! I love to learn new things and of course I want to perform my job correctly and to my manager's highest standards, so of course I'd take direction from him or her on how to do the job. Some managers can be a little more difficult to deal with than others, but it just takes a little more work to develop a relationship with them.

Can you give an example of a time when you've gotten called out for a misstep?

The employer wants to make sure you're not just saying what sounds good at the time, but that you truly understand how to manage around different cultures. Sure – at one company, I was the last one leaving the office for the day, so I went into the kitchen area, made sure the dishwasher was loaded, put soap powder in it, and turned it on to run. The following morning, I was confronted by a co-worker who demanded to know why I'd run the dishwasher when she'd already run it that afternoon? I explained I didn't know she'd already run it, that it appeared perhaps people had added dirty dishes after she ran it, so I just ran it again.

I apologized and said I wouldn't do it again. I said if it was the standard practice for that particular person to run the dishwasher at a particular time each day, it was good information to have and I certainly didn't want to complicate her life. I was always careful after that, though, not to use any of the dishes in the kitchen area unless I washed them myself by hand.

Why have you been out of work so long? You were laid off from your position at Jones Company in August of last year, and it's been about 9 months now. Are you finding it difficult to find something comparable to your previous job? Again, the interviewer here is concerned that, if they hire you, you'll only stick around as long as it takes to find a job that's more like your old job, that pays better, that has more promotion potential. You need to convince the interviewer that this blip is just that – a blip. I'm really just very picky. I don't want to accept just any job – I want to make sure whatever role I take on next, I'm able to contribute valuable expertise and knowledge. There are probably plenty of "comparable jobs" out there that I could do – but I need to know that my efforts are benefiting the company's mission and moving it forward. From what I know about Nobel and Associates, the culture is very much like I experienced at Jones, and the position you advertised closely matches my qualifications and what I'm looking for in my next role. I don't want to just be with an employer for a few months or years – I'm in it for the long-term and hope to find the right spot I'll still be able to contribute to 5 or 10 years from now.

You've been in a management role for a number of years. Why are you now interested in taking a lower level job with – obviously – a lower pay rate?

This type of move is a hard sell. Employers are always going to be suspicious of someone's desire to take a step back. After all, you're "supposed" to continue to move up to more and more responsible positions, with higher rates of pay.

If you do accept a new position without management responsibility, how will you make that transition smoothly? Employers fear hiring someone who's just looking for a way out of a bad current situation who will latch onto anything to get out.

You'll need to convince an employer your decision to step back is intentional, carefully considered and that you're committed to the change long-term. With the right reasons for making such a deliberate decision, an employer's doubts can be overcome. A year ago, my wife had a serious health scare. I thought we'd lose her. Luckily, it was a case of some medical tests being interpreted incorrectly. It became clear to me that we all only have so much time together and I wanted to make the most of my time with my family. So after a great deal of soul-searching and family discussion, I decided the time was right for me to scale back my work responsibilities and be home more. I'd been traveling three or four days a week for years, and I just didn't want to be away from my family for that long anymore. Believe me, it was not a decision I came to easily, but having made the decision, I felt a great deal of stress lifted off my shoulders. My current boss tried to find ways to reduce my workload and my travel responsibilities, but it became too easy to fall back on old habits when some crisis or other came up at work. I realized I was going to have to step completely away from my current employer in order to get the balance I needed. I know it's the right decision for me. The best part is that my new employer benefits from all my knowledge and know-how without having to pay for it.

I see that, four years ago, you made a total change in your career. What led to that decision and are you happy with the choice you made? The Interviewer wants to know a couple of things: 1) that this was a deliberate decision, not the result of being out of work; 2) that this is a direction you'll continue to follow, because they don't want to hire someone who now has 4 years of experience in a new field, only to have that person decide they liked what they were doing previously better. Yes, I did and I'm so happy I did! For the previous 6 years, I'd been taking night classes to get an Associate's degree in Electrical Engineering Technology. I had been working as a production worker in an electrical wiring factory and I saw the work the Electrical Techs and Engineers did, and knew it was something I'd be very good at. I was encouraged by the Techs and Engineers with whom I worked – they convinced me to pursue my education.

So I looked into schools and programs, settled on the one that fit me best, and dove in. I don't regret it for a minute.

My supervisor supported my pursuit of a degree throughout, and when I received my degree, I was promoted from Production Worker to Electrical Tech, with a nice bump in pay. I've spent 4 years as an Electrical Tech, and eventually I'd like to be an Engineer. I've already registered for night classes at the local University to earn a Bachelor's degree. I'll be back in school this fall.

I'd like you to know, though, that my continuing education won't have any negative impact on my ability to work a full-time job here. If anything, I become more focused and organized when I have more on my plate.

Well, since you asked, I couldn't help noticing that the tool room seems to be in disarray. I'm sure the folks who use the tools all the time know exactly where each tool belongs, but it's a little disconcerting to an outside observer. I'd totally 5S that work area, taping off areas for work benches, trash cans, and tools.

The best 5S layout I've seen is a company that photocopied the individual tools, laminated the images, cut them out and glued them in the exact space the tool should be returned to. It's the visual factory idea – it's much easier to see what's missing, and where a missing tool needs to be returned to.

Why did you leave your last job?

Short and sweet is fine – if the interviewer wants to dig deeper, s/he will continue questioning you about the reasons. <u>Unfortunately, I was terminated along with a co-worker. (or ... along with several other co-workers.)</u>

The interviewer is concerned your problems will follow you to any new job – that perhaps you don't have the skills needed for this job either. They don't want to hire someone who seems like a good fit for the job but who can't get along with others – or whatever the reason for your termination happened to be. Depending on the circumstances, you can turn this into a positive. Be honest: **"The company was going through a major reorganization and my position – along with 35 of my fellow co-workers' positions – was eliminated."**

Chapter 6: Questions on the Organization

Questions on the prospective employer are usually of significant interest to organizations during job interviews. Good answers to questions in this category have the tendency of giving an interviewee an edge over others because most people who attend job interviews are usually not prepared for them. It is imperative to remark that the best answers to questions in this category cannot come through reasoning or speculation. An interviewee easily confirms before the interviewer that he does not know the answers to the questions if he attempts them, needless to say that not attempting them does not increase the interviewee's probability of getting the job. The best answers to job interview questions in this category are usually found through an intensive research on the organization prior to the interview. This is why job seekers are advised to conduct a research on their prospective employers and their activities prior to attending a job interview. Giving the right answers to questions in this category will unarguably give a job seeker an edge over his fellow job seekers because they are usually unprepared for them.

Why do you want to work with us?

Sample Answer

Your company is unarguably the leading telecommunication company in the country. I am confident that this organization earned this wealth of enviable reputation in the highly competitive telecommunication industry because it is focused and has diligent staff. I always have passion for working with such organization, and I know that getting this job will afford me the opportunity to achieve that.

What do you know about our organization?

It is impossible to offer an impressive response to this question if you do not have prior information about the organization, especially through a research you conducted before the interview. You should not try to fabricate an answer to this question if you did not conduct a research on the organization before the job interview. Otherwise, you may end up confirming that you are merely guessing.

Sample Answer

This television house is among the earliest private television stations to be licensed in the country, but it is not among the top 10 television stations, even in the state because of the quality of the programmes it airs. One of the consequences of this is that there is low patronage from advertisers, and this is the major source of income of television houses. If I am offered appointment as the Director of Programmes in the television house, with the support of the management, I will use my wealth of experience in the media industry to revolutionise this organization.

How can you assess our organization?

Part of your research on the organization should include their major challenges, especially the advantages their competitors have over them. You may have a higher probability of being employed if you are able to comment on some of the challenges of the organization and make recommendations on how they can be addressed.

Sample Answer

Your company is one of the oldest manufacturers of powdered milk in the country. One of my observations in the attitudes of consumers is that there has been increased preference of low-price sachet powdered milk, especially among the masses who constitute the largest percentage of the consumers. But your company is yet to start packaging its products in this way. I think this is why your products are available only in the cities, but not in the rural areas because the masses there cannot afford them. I think this is an area the organization should apply an urgent change.

Do you know any of our employees?

This question may be asked because the policy of some organizations does not permit the employment of relations of their employees. In an organization that honours such policy, the probability of being employed will be low, if it is known that a relation of yours is one of their employees.

Sample Answer

To the best of my knowledge, I do not know of any relation of mine who is an employee of your organization.

How did you know about this vacancy?

If the vacancy was not advertised to the outside world, it may be difficult to know of it if you do not know any of the employees of the organization. If you allege that you do not know any of their employees, you may have to justify how you knew about the advertisement without the help of an insider.

Sample Answer

I heard of the vacancy from a friend, who is not an employee of your organization. I really do not know how he got to know about the vacancy, but I just decided to give it a trial by applying.

Can you subordinate your personal interest to that of our organization if you are employed?

This is one of the requisites for working with any organization because there will be time employees will not be able to perform official assignments without sacrificing their personal comfort and interests. You are not expected to answer this question after a second thought. Otherwise, it may be difficult for the interviewer to accept that your response is sincere (if it is in the affirmative). However, you should forget about the job if your answer is not in the affirmative. Answer the question with courage, conviction and confidence.

Sample Answer

I will always be willing to subordinate my personal interests to that of the organization because it will be practically impossible for an organization to achieve meaningful success if the employees subordinate the interest of the organization to theirs.

Do you think that you will be happy working with us?

Sample Answer

Happiness is one of the most reliable standards for measuring success. It would be irrational to apply for a job that will not increase my happiness.

Would you prefer to work with a big or small firm?

There are some merits and demerits of working with either of these organizations. If you express preference to working with a small organization while you are being interviewed by a multinational corporation, your application may be rejected. If you also express preference to working with a big organization while you are being interviewed by a small organization, it may be concluded that you will not be at home (or happy) working with the organization. You should adjust your answer to the size of the organization that is interviewing you if you truly want the job.

Sample Answers

My earliest jobs were with small organizations. I prefer working with a big organization this time because I need to advance my career by having greater challenges in an organization like yours.

I prefer working with a big organization because it offers an employee the opportunity of being exposed to global standards.

I prefer working with a small organization because it affords employees the opportunity of having a detailed knowledge of the activities of the company, unlike in big organizations where division of labour is so high that employees may not understand the inter-relationship of the activities of the various departments.

What do you love most in an Organization?

Sample Answers

I enjoy working in an organization in which the management and the employees work as a team.

I like working in an organization that does not treat some employees as sacred cows. Employees feel at home in an organization when there is no discrimination in the way the management relates with them.

How will you be an asset to our organization if you are hired?

It may be difficult to answer this question correctly if you did not conduct a prior research on the company. Emphasise how your education, experiences and professional accomplishments will guarantee an enviable success in the position you applied for.

Chapter 7: Team Success Questions

Describe a time when you had to convince a fellow student or peer to use a particular approach to an assignment. What did you say?

Why do they ask this question?

Not all of your team members will know the best approach to a particular project. You need to be able to convince them of the right approach. They might also lack the knowledge of how to do it the right way. Therefore, you have to be willing to show them the right way without making them look like fools. There might also be situations where both your approaches are right, but your approach will get the team there faster and more efficiently. Efficiency is the key to success in the big four accounting firms.

Bad Answer

I had a part-time job at a fast food restaurant one summer after school. That summer I found a way to get my line of customers moving efficiently because of a few tricks I knew on the register. One of my colleagues always had a long line with his customers yelling at him. I raised my voice and told him to learn to be more efficient. I couldn't understand why he couldn't learn the same tricks on the register that I had. It seemed simple to me.

Why this is a bad answer:
Although this shows how you operated in the team at your restaurant, it doesn't show how you contributed to team success. It just shows how you were successful yet your coworker was not. You didn't seem interested in taking the time to help him learn. You need to show how you worked in a team and ultimately achieved success through an approach that you initiated.

Good Answer

An example of a good answer to this question would be:

In college I once had a computer science class. In that class, we were given a group project where we had to code a project. During that group project, we were having a lot of difficulty coming up with a solution. Therefore, I suggested that we break up pieces of the project for each of us to solve.

One of my group members disagreed with this approach. They thought it was better if we all worked on the solution together all at one time. I didn't necessarily disagree with this approach, but I knew we would finish the project on time if we took this approach.

I told my group member that we would not finish the project by the deadline if we all worked on it at the same time. I told them that in order for all of us to be successful we had to break the project up. The group member ultimately ended up seeing my side of the argument. We split the project up, then we ended up finishing it by the deadline.

Why this is a good answer:

This is a good answer because it shows how you disagreed with a group member, but you still came to a compromise. It also shows the steps you took to get to that compromise which shows your thoughtfulness.

Describe a time when you had to work with a team to complete a project. What role did you play? What actions did you take to influence the outcome of your assignment?

Why do they ask this question?

They want to see if you are an active participant or just a follower. They also want to see if you step into the leader role. If you do take a leadership role, are you overbearing. Do you take on too much responsibility?

Bad Answer

An example of a bad answer to this question would be:
I once did a science project in high school. My group wasn't filled with the brightest people, so I just took the project over. We ended getting an A because I took over and dominated the project.

Why this is a bad answer:
This just shows that you aren't willing to trust group members and that you are judgmental. You need to show the ability to work with people of all different types of skill-sets. You can't say that you only work with the best and brightest. That makes you seem judgmental and cocky.

Good Answer

An example of a good answer to this question would
     be:
I once had a very big group project in my advanced accounting class. There were multiple parts that had to be tackled. I was co-leader with another classmate, and we both assessed everyone's likes and dislikes and doled out responsibilities based on that. We assigned

someone to research who liked to research. We assigned someone to lead the oral presentation who loved communicating. We delegated the remaining responsibilities in a similar manner. The group got along well and our final presentation was a great success. Our presentation was the most popular in the whole classroom.

Why this is a good answer:
This really shows how you work well in a team environment. You immediately jumped into the lead role and used that to help the team as a whole and not yourself.

You assessed everyone's strengths and weaknesses and delegated workloads based on that.

Describe a situation when you had to influence another student or peer to cooperate. What did you say?

Bad Answer

An example of a bad answer to this question would be:
I once had an uncooperative group member in my intermediate accounting class. In order to get him to cooperate told him to improve his attitude or else. He said that he didn't want to cooperate. Then I told him that I was going to tell the professor if you cooperate.

We ended up switching group members to address the issue.

Why this is a bad answer:
This is a bad answer because it shows that you used threats to get what you want. Instead you want to show how you can work with almost any person. You want to show how late you convince someone to come to your side. You don't want to show how you always result to threats. That's what children do.

Good Answer

An example of a good answer to this question would be:
I once had a roommate in college who was very noisy. I asked him multiple times to turn down his music. When that didn't work, I had come up with a different solution.

I ended up sitting down with him and telling him how difficult it was to deal with his noise. I told them how I would really appreciate it if you could keep the noise level to a minimum so that I could study. I was willing to work with him so that he could still listen to his music. I worked out a schedule of when he could play his music so that I could maximize my study time. He would listen to his music while I was at class. This worked out really well for us and we avoided future conflict

Why this is a good answer:
This is a good answer because it shows how you avoid a conflict. You could have yelled at your roommate or threatened him but you didn't. Instead you came up with the common solution. You didn't lose your temper. It shows that you are really interested in coming to compromise as opposed to just looking out for yourself.

Interview Question 25

What techniques have you used to gain acceptance of ideas or plans? Give me an example of a time when you used one of these techniques.

Why do they ask this question?

The big four ask this question to understand how you convince other people of your ideas and plans. That is they try to see if you even convince people at all. Maybe you don't do a lot of convincing, and you have a weakness in this area. That's what they're trying to figure out.

Bad Answer

An example of a bad answer to this question would be:
I normally just mention my ideas as they come to me, and I truly hope that people adopt my idea after the first time I mention it. I might bring up the idea one more time, but I don't really push anything. I try being nice and calm and that's how I try to convince people.

Why this is a bad answer:
Even though this might be how most people communicate, it doesn't make for good answer to this question. The best candidate that the big four want to see should have multiple skill sets to convince people of their ideas and plans. Now is that how people actually are? I don't think so, but you're going to want to make yourself seem that way to the big four.

Good Answer

An example of a good answer to this question would be:
I use multiple techniques to get people to implement my plans and ideas. I try to see things from their viewpoint before speaking to them. That way I don't offend them which will allow them to see things from my viewpoint.I also take people out for coffee, drinks,

or even a meal. When you buy people things and listen to them, they are much more willing to support you.

I'm also an active listener. I listen very attentively when people speak to me and my responses are measured and to the point. I only speak when I feel I have something to contribute and whatever I say tends to be a positive response to what the person just said.

Another technique that I use, is that if I disagree with somebody's opinion is asking questions. I ask pointed questions to where I think the weaknesses in their argument are. The questions that I ask are not offensive though. By asking questions, I hopefully get the person to see the weaknesses in their argument.

Why this is a good answer:
You detailed all your techniques that you use to get your peers to cooperate. This is also a good answer because none of the techniques are negative. You want to have at least a couple positive techniques ready. If you have only one, it will make your interviewer doubt that you really have techniques for cooperation at all.

Chapter 8: Questions to Ask

It is now your turn. As the interview draws to an end, it is almost certain that the hiring authority will ask you, "Do you have any questions for me?"

They will expect you to have some inquiries, lest you appear uninterested or unprepared.

Having queries also illuminates on your skills, qualities, and experience and will show your employer that you are the best match for the role.

As you prepare for your interview, have some questions to ask the interviewer. Remember that you are not just trying to get this position as the employers require, but forming a mutually beneficial relationship where you also assess the employer to see whether the position and the company fits you.

General tips for answering the interviewer questions include:

- Avoid focusing on "me" questions, which include those to do with salary and benefits. Remember that you are trying to showcase how you will benefit the company and not the other way around.

75

- Ask questions one by one to avoid overwhelming the interviewer.

- Avoid the YES or NO questions that can simply be answered by going through the company's website.

- Do not dwell on one point but instead ask a variety of questions to show that you are interested in learning about all aspects of the organization and the role for which you are interviewing.

- Do not ask anything too personal no matter how much you are trying to establish rapport with the person interviewing you.

- Avoid questions such as "What does this firm do?" as you are supposed to have researched that prior to the interview, or "Am I getting the job?" as you will look impatient.

- Ideally, there are three types of questions you ask the hiring manager during an interview. You ought to show your interest in the position, interest in the company, and show more about yourself.

Although you do not have to ask all questions in your list, it is advisable that you have a comprehensive list since some questions may be covered in the process of the conversation.

Questions about Position

- "How does this role contribute to larger organizational goals?"

Employers can easily find an individual to execute a role, but it is often difficult to find one that will not only carry out their role but also understand how their work connects to larger organizational goals. Such an employee is able to set standards and goals and also prioritize how to achieve and maintain valuable performance aligning with a company's growth.

This question offers you an opportunity to learn about some crucial information that may not be availed to you, especially if the company you are interviewing for is not very transparent or forthcoming. Hence, this question aims at giving you a framework to guide you if you land the role.

- "What performance metrics would you use for this role?"

Asking this question indicates that you are goal-oriented and you are ready to account for any goals concerning your work. It shows your accountability skills, which gives the employer confidence that you are out to work, not joke around.

This question helps you get the employer on their toes to figure out the actual importance of your role and communicate it to you. There are many employees out there who only have a vague picture of what their role is and yet do not exactly know what their employer wants from them.

- "What does a typical day for this position look like?"

Asking this question shows the interviewer that you want to understand the norms of your job and the daily routine to ascertain that you can manage tasks effectively and what approach you need to have if you are hired. It shows them that you are interested in knowing your schedules, planning your time, and using the day efficiently.

This question helps you align your most productive moments with your job and how to overcome challenges or handle emerging issues in the course of your work.

- "Who does this position report to?"

It goes without saying that your prospective boss will have a major impact on your career and will highly determine how productive your work is at the company. Therefore, this question shows the employers that you are keen in getting to know your immediate boss and that you look forward to establishing a proper working relationship with them.

The question helps you to gain an outlook into how the position is regarded in the company, and it will give you impressions about the management style of your job and the approach you are to give to your job if offered.

- "What are some of the challenges and roadblocks that come up in this role?"

This question shows the hiring manager your interest in the job as you have already envisioned yourself in it. It is a good sign to them that you are ready to get armed up for any stumbling blocks along the course of your work.

Asking the question helps you understand the less-appealing aspects of the job, including internal politics or difficult workmates. This information can be used to evaluate if the role is really good for you or if you are okay with the challenge.

- "Why are you hiring for this role?"

This question sends the image that you are interested in knowing the problem being solved by filling this position. It shows them that you are not a person who just indulges into a deal without knowing its source.

The question will help you if it is a new or a replacement role. A new role can indicate that the organization is growing and a replacement role would prompt some explanation as to why the previous employee left. This question will offer insight into whether there are internal promotion opportunities and even foresee any pitfalls.

- "How has this position changed over time?"

Asking this question shows that you are aware it might not be a first-time position. Someone else might have held the role, and it might have evolved. It shows them that you are interested about the future of the organization.

It is crucial to ask this question to know how it might have looked in aspects such as responsibilities. You may even get a sense of where the hiring authority feels it is going in the future. The answer can give you an unbiased insight into your role and department.

- "What is the typical career path here for a person hired into this role?"

This question shows the employer that you are not solely about reporting to work without a goal, but that you are focused and ready to be committed to your career journey. It makes them understand that you are an enlightened person who thinks about the future.

This question will provide light into how the position may advance your career and the direction it will take. It will inform your goal setting and decision making by letting you see how the employer regards career growth.

Questions about the Company

- "What do the most successful newbies do in their first thirty days here?"

This question shows the employer that you are one of a kind; you are a person who wants to get things going as soon as they hit the ground. It is also a good indicator that you are interested in the patterns of success and that you are willing to replicate a successful performer.

This question helps you gauge the unspoken expectations of the company and the specific environment. In case you land the job, this question would prevent you from suffering the case of "I wish I knew then what I know now" six months down the line.

- "What biggest challenge has the team faced in the past year?"

Most often interviewers will paint a pleasant picture of what joining the workforce looks like, some of which you will have to face and help to address once you join. This question shows the interviewer that you are organized and like to prepare for handling challenges.

This question also helps you to know if you will take the job if the offer comes or not. It also opens up your mind into some of the techniques used by the workers to overcome challenges.

- "Why did you decide to work at this organization?"

This question is a chance for the interviewer to talk about themselves and also sell the organization.

It offers insight into what motivated your prospective workmate and what would most probably be good for you if their motivators align with what interests you in a job.

- "What keeps you motivated working in this company in the time you have stayed here?"

First, this is an indicator that you have already studied your interviewer and you know they have been in the company for a while. Showing that you are interested in knowing the taste of the people who work in the company is impressive.

This question helps you learn about your prospective company's workplace flexibility, career growth opportunities, and leadership opportunities.

- "Where do the staff members take lunch?"

This is a relaxed question that you can ask to break the hard atmosphere and create a conversation about shared interests.

It would not hurt knowing a little about the company's culture and lunch suggestions for the future in case you get the job. You would learn if the staff take time to go out, if people eat in groups, or whether they eat at their desks because they are too busy to socialize.

- "What is this company's customer service attitude?"

This question is impressive as it shows your interest in making a connection between how the customer service is delivered with the ultimate result. Typically, how customers or clients are treated daily indicates how productivity is attained.

This question helps you to hear in a better way some information you could have attained an idea about from the company's website. It also helps you in making the decision about accepting the job if offered a chance or to decline, especially if your prospective position is that in which you will be communicating with customers directly.

- "How would you describe this company's values?"

This question shows the employer that you want to know the fundamental value framework that guides the operations of the company. It shows them that you like to prepare in advance to conduct yourself in line with the basic guidelines of behavior.

This question allows you to know the basic standards of conduct expected in the company.

- "Could you please tell me some of the tangible traits of successful people among the staff?"

This question shows that you are interested in attaining an outlook of what success is in the company. It pushes the hiring authority to think about their top performer.

The response to this question gives you an idea of what it takes to be a star candidate and generally how to impress your employer.

- "Which manners do the people who struggle most on the job display?"

This question shows the hiring authority that you are a straightforward individual who is trying to attain a concrete idea of what to do and what not to do if you get hired. It is impressive because it portrays you as a candidate who is confident about asking tough questions.

This question response offers you an idea of what poor performance looks like, which will inform your decision making and standards setting. You will also see how your employer handles such a tough question.

- "How is negative feedback delivered?"

This tough question is important as it showcases your confidence levels and shows that you are interested in learning how the team works. It also tells them that you are a mature person who expects some negative feedback if things go wrong.

It helps you know how people react to negative feedback differently and how your employer is likely to give negative feedback. You will learn if the negative feedback is given differently depending on who is asking or whether feedback is a two-way approach. Therefore, you will know if you are able to work with them.

Questions about Yourself

- "Do you have any queries about my qualifications?"

This question sends a positive light of you to your interviewer since it shows that you welcome feedback. It shows that you understand yourself and would be willing to work and improve on yourself. It gives the hiring authority a chance to ask you about anything you might have mentioned in your résumé and was not portrayed in your conversation, and which may be holding them back from hiring you.

This question offers you a chance to make clarifications about concerns face to face without confrontations.

- "What should I expect to wear on the first day to work?"

Dress code is among the touchy subjects of an interview since you want to show that you are concerned about following the company culture but you do not want to show you might have wardrobe malfunctions. It is important to ask this question, especially if business wear has not been your thing.

This question helps you get the firsthand information from the human resources manager about the company culture.

- "How much travel is expected?"

It is important to know if regular travel is expected for a prospective job and to establish if you are able to travel as much as the job requires. It shows the employer that you like being organized, clarifying that even though you like to travel, you would like to know how often and where you have to travel.

Asking your employer this question helps to inform your decision on whether to accept the job if offered or whether to decline. It will help you relate the obligations at hand and how flexible you are to travel.

- "Is relocation a possibility?"

This question shows the employer that you are mindful of the job posting process to avoid inconveniencing both your family if you have one and the organization too.

Response to this question gives you an idea of the location you are being posted to and to determine whether you will relocate or not. The employer will also give you an outlook of the relocating process and expenses for you to plan ahead if you are extended the offer.

- "If I am extended a job offer, how soon would you like me to start?"

This is one of the most important questions to ask at a job interview. It shows the employers that you do not just assume things, especially issues that might affect your schedule and make you fail in fulfilling a commitment.

Response to this question will give you a glimpse into how essential the position you are applying for is to the operations of the company. Even if you have not gotten the job offer yet, it is good to think about a tentative time frame for hitting the ground if you get the job.

- "When should I expect to get a response from you?"

Asking this question reaffirms your interest in talking to employers after your interview. It also indicates that you are confident about being a good match for the role.

Response to this question helps you to assess the level of importance this role has to the organization, and also whether it is most likely good news or bad news that you will be receiving. Although you may not get a definite answer, you will get an idea of how long the employer takes to respond to job candidates.

- "Are there any other questions I can answer for you?"

This question shows your recruiter that you are keen to explain all details they may want to clarify. It shows them that you accord them their status by giving them a chance to ask you any other remaining issue of concern.

The question also gives you a chance to reaffirm your interests in the position, reiterate your skills and abilities, and to show the interviewer why you are worth the position. It also helps you gauge the interviewer's final thoughts as the interview comes to an end.

Chapter 9: Questions You Should Not Ask at the Interview

The following are examples of some questions that you should never ask during your interview:

1. Can I do this job at home?

If you are interviewing for a job that is a freelance position, then the job advertisement would have mentioned it. If you ask the interviewer about working from home, then you imply that you don't like to work with other people. You also don't like to be supervised and have a difficult work schedule. Sometimes, the option is given to work from home, but you should never assume that the same opportunity will be given to you.

2. What does your company do?

You should never ask the company about what they do if there is information readily available on the web about it. We should emphasize that you need to do your research on the company beforehand and gather as much information as possible. If you have not done your homework beforehand, the interviewer will assume that you are not actually interested in the job.

3. How much vacation time do we have?

If you ask about vacation, then you're going to imply that you are a lazy employee who is not committed to the job and that you will not be an effective worker. This could be a red flag for the company that is interviewing you.

4. Did I get the position?

When you ask this question, you put the employer in an uncomfortable situation, and it makes you look like you are impatient. Instead of asking this question, you should ask when you are likely to hear back about the position. Ask a question such as the following: *Do you have multiple rounds of interviews? When will I likely hear back about the position?*

5. How many hours do you have to work for this job? Will I need to be available to work on the weekend?

If you talk about the hours of work, you show that you want to work as little as possible. Instead of asking about the amount of work hours, you should ask a question like, "What is the typical workday like?" This will talk about what kind of commitment you will give to the job.

6. How long would I need to wait before getting a promotion?

If you ask this question, you imply that you are not actually interested in this position, but would rather like to move on to the next level. Instead of asking about this, you should ask for the opportunities for professional development and growth within a company.

7. What kinds of benefits are offered to employees?

Questions about benefits, such as health insurance, should wait until after you have received a firm job offer from the company. If you need to have a certain benefit, then you should talk to an HR person rather than the interviewer.

8. How long is lunch?

You should not ask how long lunch is, because then you are implying that you don't want to work a lot and that you would rather play than be an ideal employee.

9. How late can I arrive to work before getting sacked?

You don't want to ever talk about arriving late to work. It is simply unprofessional. Arriving late to work shows you don't care about your job or the consequences of it. You should try to be on time every day.

10. Does this company monitor internet usage?

If you ask this question, you are implying you have something to hide in your Internet usage, which could be a red flag for the interviewer. It is important that you steer clear of this question at all costs.

11. What warnings do you receive before getting fired?

This question is also a red flag, because it shows that you might go all the way with something or try to get away with whatever it is before getting fired. Don't ask this question ever.

12. Do you check references? Do you conduct background checks?

If you ask this question, you will reveal that you have something to hide. So, you should not ask.

13. Do you have security cameras watching all that I do?

This question assumes that you may not be trustworthy and therefore would not be a good candidate for the company.

14. Will the company monitor my activities on Facebook?

You should assume that your online profile is public and that information revealed on it will be available to your employer. Try to refrain from posting any racy material on the web because it could end up getting you fired from a job.

15. Is it always noisy in this place?

This question would give a bad impression, because it would show that the working environment is not suitable for you. Try not to ask this question.

16. How soon can I get a raise?

This shows that you are more interested in money rather than the job itself. You should not ask questions related to money or salary at the interview, especially the first one.

Conclusion

It is clear that there are some questions that are just best not to ask as they indicate red flags that could make the interviewer question your ability to join the team. Even if you cruise through the rest of the interview and answer the questions thrown at you, it is still possible to mess everything up if you ask the wrong interview questions, so don't blow your chances by asking unacceptable things.

Chapter 10: Behavior-Based Questions

Preparation

Many of the behavioral questions aim to find out how you respond to negative situations. You should have a number of examples that show how you faced some negative situation and had a positive outcome.

Identify seven or eight examples of situations from your previous jobs where you exhibited the skills that employers usually seek in a candidate. Think of examples that bring forth your best skills and behaviors.

Half of the examples you choose should be positive and show your accomplishments and situations where you met your goals.

Half of them should be examples of situations that were initially negative but ended positively.

Your examples should be from different areas of life.

Use examples that are quite recent.

Techniques

There are various techniques that you can use for answering behavioral questions. They are:

STAR: This is mostly for interviews where you are asked questions related to your competencies, skills, interests, values, and personality. You are expected to support the answers with some sort of evidence. You can use the STAR method to answer questions based on competency and to provide that evidence.

Situation: You should briefly describe the who, where, and when.

Task: You can give an outline of the task and the objective.

Action: Describe your actions. You must focus on the role you played and your contribution.

Result: Explain the result or outcome and the skills it helped you to develop.

Use this format to create a wide variety of examples. Take these examples from various situations in your career.

CAR: "C" stands for context or challenge, "a" stands for action, and "r" stands for result. First, describe the problem or the task that had to be dealt with. Next talk about how you responded. Finally, explain the outcome of your response.

OKEYO: This technique involves: giving an overview, explaining the key events, describing your role, and detailing the outcome or result.

PAR: First, talk about the problem, then describe the action you took, and finally, explain the Result.

Sample Questions

Here are some sample behavior-based questions that are asked in interviews. They are related to various areas such as leadership, problem solving, communication, and teamwork.

Leadership

- Describe an occasion where your achievements were vital to the success of a project.

- Tell us about an occasion where you took charge of a situation, sought out support, and achieved positive results.

- Tell us about an occasion where you disciplined or fired a friend.

- Describe an occasion where you had to help leaders grow under your guidance.

- Describe an occasion where you were disappointed in your behavior.

Initiative

- Tell us about some situation where you had to overcome obstacles to accomplish your objectives.

- Describe one of your goals that you are trying to achieve now.

- Give an example of an important contract that you won or lost.

- Describe a situation where you helped implement a new program.

- Tell us about a scenario where your actions played a significant role in the success of a goal.

Problem Solving

- Give an example of a situation where it was necessary to analyze the facts quickly, state the key issues clearly, and either respond instantly or make a plan for the future.

- If you had to perform that task once again, how would you respond differently?

- Describe a situation where you missed the obvious solution for a problem.

- Tell us about a scenario where you were able to anticipate the problems and take preventive measures.

- Give an example of a situation where you overcome a big obstacle.

Communication

- Tell us about an occasion when you successfully presented one proposal to a person of authority.

- Give an example of a situation where you persuaded someone to use your idea.

- Describe a situation where you persuaded the members of your team to listen to your ideas. What was the effect?

- Tell us about an occasion where you showed tolerance toward some opinion that differed from your own.

Work in an Effective Manner with Others

- Tell us about an occasion where you motivated others to get the desired result.

- Give an example to show that you have been successful in maintaining a productive relationship with others despite having different views.

- Describe how you handled a tough situation with your coworker.

- Tell us about a situation in where you helped to get your work group or team back on track.

Work Quality

- Give an example of a situation where a report that you had written was positively received. Why do you think that was?

- Tell us about an occasion where a report you had written was not received well. What do you think was the problem?

- Describe a specific program or project you worked on that brought about an improvement in an important area of work.

- Tell us about an occasion where you fixed some objectives that were too high.

Innovation and Creativity

- Give an example of an occasion where you found a new and better way to do something.

- Describe a situation where you solved a problem creatively.

- Tell us about an occasion where you came up with novel ideas that proved to be helpful to the successful implementation of a project.

- Give an example of a situation where it was necessary for you to make the others use their creativity.

Priority Setting

- Give an example of a situation where you successfully maintained a balance between competing priorities.

- Tell us about an occasion where you were expected to choose the most vital aspects of an activity and ensure that they were completed.

- Describe a scenario where you successfully prioritized the various elements of some complicated project.

- Give an example of an occasion where you became caught up in the various details of some project.

Decision Making

- Tell us about an occasion where you were required to make an important decision but had very few facts.

- Give an example of a situation where you had to make an unpopular decision.

- Describe an occasion where you had to adjust to a difficult situation. How did you handle it?

- Explain a time where you made the wrong decision.

- Tell us about an occasion where you fired or hired a wrong person.

Work in Various Conditions

- Describe a situation where you worked well under pressure.

- Give an example of a project that you could not complete in time.

- Give an example of an occasion when it was necessary for you to change the work midway because of a change in organizational priorities.

- Describe how you deal with stressful situations.

Delegation of Work

- Tell us about an occasion where you effectively delegated a project.

- Give an example of an occasion where you did not delegate work properly.

- Describe a situation where you had delegate work to someone who already had a big workload. How did you handle it?

Customer Service

- Give an example of a time where you had to deal with an irate client.

- What programs related to customer service that you have participated in are you proudest of?

- Have you ever made a lasting impression on a customer? When?

STAR Method Sample Answers

Question: Describe a time when you were under pressure but successfully completed the job.

Step 1: Situation

When I was working on my previous job, my coworker suddenly left for personal reasons. He had been taking care of a very important project. Now there was no manager for it.

Step 2: Task

The task was handed over to me by my supervisor. There was no concession regarding the deadline. The project, which required several weeks time to be completed, had to be done in a few days time.

Step 3: Action

I asked that my weekly workload be reduced so that I could focus on this task. I delegated these weekly goals to my teammates.

Step 4: Result

I dedicated more time for the project and completed it accurately and on time. My efforts and attitude were appreciated by my supervisor. After that, my responsibilities were increased. Eventually, I got a promotion and my salary was raised.

Question: Give an example of a situation where you were the team leader.

Step 1: Situation

I was working as the software developer for a company. There were six members on my team. We were developing a novel finance module that would be used for the core accounting products of our company.

Step 2: Task

It was a critical project, and the launch dates were fixed. Quite a large sum of money had been invested in advertising the products. The work on this project was very slow and very little time was left when the leader fell sick and had to take time off work.

Step 3: Action

When I was in school, I was the captain of the sports team. I enjoyed the challenges and responsibilities involved in leadership. Therefore, I offered to take the responsibility for the project. Using my skills for technical analysis, I spotted some minor mistakes in the basic coding. I saw that the mistakes caused sporadic errors that slowed down the work.

I negotiated with my product director and arranged for a bonus incentive. We decided to give pizzas to the team members who worked in the evenings to make corrections in the coding. In this way I was able to speed up the work.

Step 4: Result

Although the cost of the project went up slightly because of this bonus, we reached the target in time. The additional cost was negligible in comparison to the loss we would have incurred if there was a delay in launching the product. Besides this, it would have a negative impact on the product branding. Moreover, the team members were delighted to get the bonus. As a consequence, I have been promoted and have become the official team leader.

CAR Method Sample Answers

Question: Tell us about an occasion when you solved some major problem in your company.

Step 1: Context

A major event was going to be held in the company, and a colleague of mine had arranged with for an overseas supplier to provide the materials. He had chosen the shipping date as the same date of the event. He did not consider the time that would be needed to clear customs and get the things transported to the event location. It was obvious that it would not be possible to get the supplies in time for the event. He was very upset and asked me to help.

Step 2: Action

I found out that similar materials were available in another city and could be transported by train. I asked him to cancel the shipping order and contacted another supplier who agreed to send the materials to the local railway station two days ahead of the event. After the materials arrived at the railway, we used trucks to transport them to the event location.

Step 3: Result

The materials arrived on time, and the event was successful.

Question: Give an example of a situation where you had to demonstrate initiative.

Step 1: Context

When I started at my previous job, the phone was used to handle all of the requests related to customer service. This took up the staff's valuable time. In addition, errors occurred in the quotes and documentation that caused further delays and customer satisfaction, among other issues.

Step 2: Action

I wanted to rectify this, so I took the initiative to develop an automate workflow system. The customers had to fill in a form and make the service request online. They would provide all the information required. This minimized the documentation errors. The service requests were reviewed daily, and the details were automatically added to the database.

Step 3: Result

The staff did not have to spend time taking calls. This reduced the labor costs and improved the productivity by 20%. Additionally, the turnaround time and customer satisfaction rates improved. The system helped to save time as well as resources, and it was so successful that it was used in the company locations.

Question: Tell us about an occasion where you organized a large event.

Step 1: Context

While working as a personal assistant in my previous job, I was given the responsibility to organize a seminar for the management team. Plenty of planning and attention to details were needed for this task. I had to find a venue; make arrangements for speakers, catering, and accommodations; take care of the finances; and communicate with the stakeholders.

Step 2: Action

I wrote down all of the things that needed to be done and then made checklists. I recorded the names of the people involved and their contact details. I sent daily reminders to them through email and phone regarding specific tasks. By following this detailed and strict schedule, I ensured everything was on the right track. I was able to see how much work had been completed and make sure nothing was forgotten.

Step 3: Result

The seminar went on very smoothly. All the attendees were highly satisfied, and I received positive feedback. Since I had been successful in organizing this function, I was given the responsibility to plan other events for the company. This expanded my role as an organizer.

Question: Describe an occasion where you had to overcome some challenging situation.

Step 1: Context

While working at my previous job, the company went through a difficult situation. I was given the responsibility to reduce expenditure and save money in a short time span.

Step 2: Action

To fulfil this task, I looked at various options that would help reduce the costs. I considered reducing the headcount, cutting departmental budgets, freezing wages, changing the company's accounts policies, and examining capital structure. I analyzed the cost-benefit for each alternative and evaluated the long- and short-term consequences, as well as the risks.

Step 3: Result

It was not easy to lay off the staff, but it was necessary. I made a number of changes to the company's expenditures and allowed a few of the employees to work part-time. In this way, I managed to save money without negatively impacting the company's operations or staff morale.

Question: Tell us about an occasion where you demonstrated adaptability.

Step 1: Context

I worked as the project leader for my company's marketing campaign. By coincidence, a week before launch one of our competitors launched a similar campaign. If we continued with our initial plans and launched our campaign the following week, it would look as if we had copied them even though we had worked on the project for weeks before they launched theirs.

Step 2: Action

I understood that it was necessary to make some changes to maintain our originality. I called all of the team members for a meeting and a brainstorming session. We had already done all of the research, so we only needed to come up with fresh ideas to make the content look different without changing our goals.

I quickly modified the old plan and delegated the work to the different team members create new content. I also engaged a freelancer to produce high quality content. All of us worked long hours that week and completed the project on time.

Step 3: Result

Our campaign was very successful. The new content was much better than the original plan. We were happy that we could quickly modify the plan and deliver a great campaign.

Chapter 11: Describe how you work.

You might have heard something about work style. This is a really common kind of question, but there are many people that just don't know how to answer effectively. When it comes to this question, you'll want to avoid talking about your personality in this question. They just want to know how you get through the day.

You might feel tempted to say that you're laid back when it comes to work, but this answer will really just work against you. Being laid back is really a personality trait, and it's not a necessarily desirable trait when it comes to work. No one wants an employee that just kind of meanders around at work. They want to make sure that you're going to give them the most for their money.

You'll also want to avoid saying that you're not a fan of conflict. This doesn't really have a lot to do with your work style. This answer doesn't really tell the interviewer anything about your work style.

For a good answer, there are a couple things you will want to do. You will want the answer that you give to mesh with the job that you're applying for. If you've got a very straight forward, data-driven position, then you won't want to spend time talking about the creative solutions that you're able to come up with. It isn't a necessary trait for your job.

You'll want to address whether you like to work in groups or by yourself. You might have an actual preference, but you'll also want to address what this particular job requires of you. Being able to work both alone and with someone else can be a great bonus for most companies. Talk about how comfortable with both.

You'll also want to tell them about how much instruction you need on jobs. This is something that you should be upfront with, especially if you tend to only function well with a lot of instruction or very little instruction. This can help see if this job will be a good fit for you. The boss might be on the other side of the spectrum from you. Without being upfront, you could be stuck in a job where you aren't able to function at your most effective.

With this kind of question, you'll want to touch on the strengths you have that fit well with this job. You might talk about organization, planning, performance, and more. These are just ideas to get you thinking. Regardless of the exact answer, you will want to approach these questions with a prepared, strategic answer that will not only address the question, but that will touch on other parts of your personality and work style that make you a good fit for the job.

In one word, describe yourself.

When you get to this kind of question, you have to understand what the interviewer is trying to do: get inside your head. Hiring is a gamble. Companies always worry about who they're hiring. The person that hires you also has an interest in how well you go because they can be blamed if you aren't a good hire.

So you'll want to refer to the four basic questions to help inform your answer: Are you capable of doing the job? Do you have an understanding of the job? Will you be able to do the job? Do you pose a risk to this person's continued employment?

If you don't do well in this position, you'll find yourself posing quite a huge risk to another person. So in order to get an idea of how well you will do, they ask some odd questions like this one.

There are a lot of words to pick from. There's dynamic, motivated, successful, responsible, strategic, dedicated, creative, flexible, reliable, dependable, fair, helpful, valuable, enthusiastic, organized, steady, focused, honest, and many more words that you could use to describe yourself. This is a really hard question to pin down.

Personally, I use 'dynamic.' This word works because I'm adaptive and do whatever is necessary to succeed. It's an all-purpose word that applies to many different jobs. However, I want you to avoid just picking a word for yourself. You'll need to think about your job and the kind of words that might fit well with this job.

Every answer that you give is hopefully leading you to a job offer. So you will need to be aware at every point. Don't think about this question as just about who you and what you are like, but focus on how you can relate that back to the job. You might pick a trait that will help you stand out from the rest of the applicants. You might want to use 'bright' because you're quite smart, but 'successful' will probably be a better fit for the employer.

Other good words include responsible, dependable, creative, flexible, strategic, dedicated, motivated, valuable, enthusiastic, organized, steady, focused, honest, fair, helpful, and reliable. Regardless of what you want to pick, think about the job and what kinds of traits are good for someone in this particular position. Be aware that this question can also be followed by a request for an explanation or example that shows off this trait, so you'll want to be prepared with at least one story that can show off the word that you have chosen.

Do you like working alone or with a time?

This question is fairly common, but that doesn't mean that it isn't a tricky one to deal with. While they are asking about your preference, there are few jobs that you will find that don't have you working both in a team and alone at some point. That's where the tricky nature of this question comes into play. You might actually prefer one, but saying so will cause you more problems. Being comfortable with both work styles is really important for many jobs.

There are some standard answers, such as, "I work well both ways. I do great when I work as a team, but I'm also comfortable when working alone." However, you'll really want to see if you can improve this answer. In order to improve it, you will need to know a little bit about the job that you are trying to get into. You'll need to know what is typically part of the job. This might be research that you complete ahead of the interview or things that you might know from working similar jobs.

So after looking at the job, you might be able to use an answer like, "I typically prefer working alone; however, working with a team can help creatively because we can bounce ideas around and it helps us learn from each other" or "I usually prefer to work in a group, but having a part of a project that is my own is also nice at times."

Both of these answers get at your preference without being outright negative about the other side of the situation. This positivity is extremely important. A hiring manager will feel much more confident hiring someone that is confident and positive. Flexibility is a desirable attribute in people.

However, we suggest that you don't just stop at answering the question. Ask them a question back about the situation like, "Roughly how much time is spent working with a time versus time I will spend working on my own?" You can ask about the kind of environment that the business encourages. This allows you to not only learn more about the situation but also keeps the conversation going.

Have you had to conform to a policy that you did not agree with? Tell me about that time.

We have discussed behavioral interview questions already. The key to the answer is usually the STAR (situation or task, action, result) structure for the story, but this question is one that you don't want to have a good story about. This question is possibly worse than asking you about a difficult situation that you handled. This one prevents you from looking like you overcame something. Instead, it's showing you in possibly one of your lowest moments. You're not going to look good during this question.

You'll want to think carefully about your answer to this kind of question. What made you not conform at first with the policy? What made you conform in the end? You may think of yourself as some sort of martyr in the situation, but someone else might not see that. In fact, if the policy was bad enough, you might come out looking pretty bad.

You might have known something that your previous boss didn't know, but that doesn't make you look good either. That's getting close to badmouthing your former employer. That's something you should definitely avoid. In fact, that kind of answer might get you in trouble with your new boss or even prevent you from getting into this new job.

When you get to the heart of the matter, most people can't really affect the policies at their work. All of those rules are set up by someone else and you can't do much to influence them. Even if you bring information to the table, you might not be able to change anything or get a message across. If you don't comply, you could lose your job.

With this answer, you'll have to be careful. This question is hard, but it's also giving the potential employer a lot of good information. They're wanting to know how you communicated, whether or not you confronted your boss, and if you managed to avoid the situation entirely.

The best answer might simply be, "Sorry, I can't recall that happening in my previous jobs." Of course, this might not be enough to stop the interviewer. If they press, you can follow up with, "If this happened, I would probably ask questions or express my concern. It is part of my job to support the rest of the team. That included bringing potential issues into the light so they can be dealt with before they actually become problems. However, the decision belongs to my supervisor in the end." You are showing that you think critically, work with the team, and respect authority. This kind of answer can be really attractive to potential employers.

Describe a time where you believe you went beyond the call of duty.

This is the best kind of question to get. It's a behavioral interview question, but this kind of question really gives you a chance to shine. This is the kind of story that you should always have on hand. Exceeding expectations is always a good thing to talk about. This shows that you bring quite a bit of value when you work.

You should always have a story prepared before you go into the interview. Try to pick one that will speak to the job that you are applying for, not just the job that you have had in the past. Speaking of what you can offer in the future is always a good choice. You can focus on particular skills or tasks that might be in your future with this job. The situation should be a little bit difficult. Conflict and resolution are always part of a good narrative.

The general story should follow this outline, "We needed (blank) done. There were some specific tasks that we needed to do. I did X, Y, and Z. These were the results of the situation."

This is just following the STAR method. It will really help you get the most out of your story. Don't feel like you have to hold back or not brag. This is a situation where you are meant to brag. This will help you show off your best qualities and also show you communicate well. You can even provide a 'brag book' which will be a physical representation of what you did and show all of the proof of what you did. Combine a good story with the book and you'll have major points in this interview.

If you were made to choose to become any animal in the planet, what would your choice be, and why would you pick it?

While a job interview tends to be a formal affair, there are some interviewers who are fond of throwing the prospective applicants a few curveballs. Their reasoning behind this can vary. Some think that your answer to such an odd question would reveal much about you. Others may just want to find out your reaction when confronted with an unexpected situation, like being asked such a question out of the blue. Whatever reason the interviewer has for asking, these questions do offer a hint into how you think, and these questions can be seen as opportunities to display your wit and quick thinking. After all, when you head into an interview, you should be prepared for anything they may throw your way. One of the better methods to get in the right mindset for an interview is to think about what qualities and attributes are most suited to the job you're seeking. If you're able to identify this, you'll have a much easier time answering any type of question appropriately. You can use this insight to prepare answers on how who you are as a person, your personality, your skills, or even your hobbies make you well-suited for the job.

For this specific type of question, picking a specific animal isn't really important, but rather, making sure that you can link your choice and the attributes needed for the job is. Of course, it would be best to avoid picking animals that already have negative attributes associated with them, like bugs, snakes, or even chickens. Once you've made your choice, you have to start explaining the reasoning behind it. You should link yourself to the animal, explaining the similarities that you find. Some examples would be liking yourself to an eagle, at least if you're going for a higher position, but that comparison may be unfavorable for jobs that need lots of cooperation. Horses are also a good choice, as they are strong and hard workers, who function just as well solo or as part of a bigger group. Ants are diligent and known as tenacious and hard workers, as well as being one of the best team players in the animal kingdom. Dogs are known for their loyalty and friendliness, which may suit certain roles. Many other animals may prove to be good choices to display your chosen attributes, just make sure you are able to link them properly. If the interview is going well, you may even be able to end it on a light note by asking your interviewer what he would choose if the question was posed to him.

If you could rewind the clock, repeating the last ten years, how would you choose to do things?

This is a question that invites much thought. After all, we tend to have many regrets, big and small. We may regret speeding that one time on a country road, investing in a bad portfolio, buying a bad outfit, or any number of other things we wish we didn't do. However, when it comes to this question being posed during an interview, the interviewer is most likely thinking of something else. This question is in fact designed to make you reveal what you feel your weaknesses are. This question tends to draw out your flaws, as they can see that based on what you regret. This question may be a good opportunity to address any possible issues you had in your past work history, and in fact, this question may be triggered by their knowledge of such issues. For example, if they see that you have had a previous employment that lasted for a suspiciously short time before you left, this may pique their interest enough to ask the question. You can explain this in a diplomatic manner, perhaps saying that you regret quitting your job to take another, saying that it didn't turn out to be a good move, but when it happened, it was the best decision you felt you could make with the information you had available. You can follow that up saying that regardless, you learned much from it, but if you knew what would happen, you wouldn't have done it. Try to frame issues as positively as you can, but do not lie. If you lie, you're out of the running for sure.

If your career has been on the smooth side, and there are no incidents to really explain, then you may be able to answer this with a lighter note. If you want to be more serious when answering however, you can say that while everyone has regrets, decisions and choices that they wish they could reverse, you are happy with the general direction and trajectory of your life, both career-wise and personal. That answer is fairly neutral, while showing the interviewer that you have not really made any major mistakes that you truly wish you could reverse, and that answer will most likely do its job in most situations.

Chapter 12: Salary Questions

Getting the amount of money you deserve is truly an art, because of two conflicting agendas: Employers want to hire you as cheaply as they can, while you want to get as much as you can. Timing is oh so important, so delay discussing salary until you receive a job offer, when you're in the strongest bargaining position (even if you're chomping at the bit to find out what it pays). The interviewer will never want you more than he or she does at that moment.

Whoever mentions a number first loses in this game, and both the interviewer and job-hunter can jostle to get the other to show their hand. Be strategic and dance around a bit with your responses, ask for more information, display thoughtful silence, and utter the immortal words: "Is that the best you can do?" Often interviewers have "wiggle room" with salaries, and can pay more if you convince them you deserve it. Learning how to use classic negotiation techniques is invaluable in upping your ante in obtaining the best salary.

What are your expectations regarding promotions and salary increases? How much do you expect if we offer this position to you? Or: What salary are you looking for? Or: What is your salary requirement?

I want to understand the job duties and responsibilities completely, so I don't know at the moment. What do similar jobs at the company pay?

What the interviewer is asking/looking for: If the interviewer asks this in your first interview, he or she may hope you give a figure outlandishly high or ludicrously low, which either way will knock you out of serious consideration. Or a figure that will steer the interviewer toward an end of the range the employer is willing to pay, or set a figure if the amount has not yet been decided. If asked much later in the interview process—perhaps after three interviews—the interviewer may be ready to offer you the job.

Good answer: Avoid giving a number as long as you can. Say you want to make sure you understand the job duties and responsibilities completely, and tick off what you know one by one. Then try to counter with your own question, like the salary range the interviewer is allowed to consider for the job, what similar jobs at the company pay, or what he or she thinks someone with your qualifications and skills will command. Stall by saying that without knowing all the details about benefits, it's hard to cite a figure.

If throwing the ball back into the interviewer's court doesn't work and you are pressed to give a number, offer a salary range that reflects your research about this type of job before the interview. ("Help wanted" ads, employees in this job type, trade associations, and salary information websites can be helpful.) The low end should be the minimum you want to accept. Of course, you may already know the salary being offered from an ad or the recruiter who told you about this job.

Bad answer: Blurting out a figure that may knock you out of the running for being too high or too low, or box you into a figure, instead of seeing the question as the negotiating gambit it is. Or saying salary doesn't matter, you just need a job. Never show an interviewer you're desperate—your value will go down in his or her eyes.

How much are you worth?

I feel I deserve at least $xxx pa due to my qualifications and career accomplishments.

What the interviewer is asking/looking for: The interviewer wants you to make a case for the salary you want and match up your qualifications with the job requirements.

Research what you're worth online. Salary, com shows salary ranges for jobs in many industries by years of experience, metro area, and zip code. Career Journal, com, a Wall Street Journal site, shows median salaries by job title, industry, and city. Jobstar.org links to over 300 salary surveys in many different industries.

Good answer: Be aware of the market rate for this job from your research in the salary range you name, and confident you meet all of the job qualifications, which you list, if not more.

Bad answer: An answer that shows you are operating in the dark, with little or no knowledge about what the going rate for this job is. A naive job-hunter is usually an underpaid job-hunter.

What are you making now? Or: What was your salary in your last job?

My last job was totally different so it does not matter.

What the interviewer is asking/looking for: Sadly, many interviewers are unduly influenced by your last salary, and use it as a guide to offering you a similar salary, or a bit more.

Good answer: Say that you feel your current (or last) salary shouldn't be relevant to the salary for this job, since they are different. Perhaps you are coming from the public or nonprofit sector, which often pay less, started the job at a low base, or there were budget cuts, **etc.** If pressed, and you know you were underpaid, you can include the dollar value of benefits like health insurance, profit sharing, stock options, and salary instead of vacation in your figure. Just be able to justify it if asked why it doesn't match your pay stub.

Bad answer: A flat figure, with no explanation if it's underpaid, which tempts the interviewer to tie a salary offer to your last salary.

Sometimes interviewers ask to see payroll stubs or W-2 tax forms when you are hired, or condition the job offer on salary verification with your employer or an outside agency. Your signature on a job application with the tiny print gives them permission. So don't invent a figure you can't justify.

What is your salary history?

I don't know, I need some time to figure out.

What the interviewer is asking/looking for: He or she wants to know how often you received raises and promotions, and how much, for clues to how well you did on the job to decide on the salary to offer you.

Good answer: Frequent and sizable jumps in salary look good, obviously, so why not admit it if this is the case? If not, or if you don't want your salary history to influence the salary offer, dodge it by saying it will require some time to figure out. If the interviewer expects you to do so, respond that you will do it as soon as you go home. If pressed to do it on the spot, okay.

Bad answer: Lack of steady, upward progress, which makes the interviewer willing to lowball the salary offer or gives him or her second thoughts about you.

Don't ask what salary the job pays. This pegs you as someone too interested in money and not enough in the job. Wait for the interviewer to bring up salary.

You've been stuck at the same salary in the same job for the past few years: How come? Or: Why aren't you making more money at your age?

Unfortunately, the advancement opportunities were severely limited at my employer due to budget constraints, so that is why I am here.

What the interviewer is asking/looking for: The interviewer shouldn't know this—hopefully, you didn't volunteer this, or perhaps the ad, application, or interviewer insisted nobody would be considered without a complete salary history. He or she is wondering if your lack of steady upward progress signals something sinister about your job performance, like laziness or lack of motivation.

Good answer: Note that advancement opportunities were severely limited at your employer, due to budget constraints or employees with more seniority. Segue quickly to this is why you are job-hunting, and eager to apply your skills and expertise to this particular job.

Bad answer: Shame, defensiveness, or anything that shows you are not a desirable commodity this employer should snap up.

That's too high for us. Can you come down a little?

Yes, I can. No problem.

What the interviewer is asking/looking for: He or she is interested, but wants you at a somewhat lower price.

Good answer: Cite a lower range that you are willing to accept. While negotiating up can be hard (because lowballing your salary can trap you), negotiating down is much easier. You should always ask for more money than you expect to get, because you have a better chance of ending up with the amount you expect even if you lower your demand. You can also ask for the benefits or perquisites to be sweetened if you do well in a few months, instead of money up front—for example, a performance review with a raise and/or promotion, a bonus, more vacation or comp time, **etc.**

Bad answer: You are not willing to budge, because the figure or range you cited was your absolute minimum.

Never mention a fixed number. It will box you in, perhaps knock you out of the running if it's too high, or peg you as a cheap hire if too low. Cite a salary range instead, if pressed. If job applications ask for desired salary, write "open" or "competitive."

How about a salary of (fill in the blank)?

Is that the best you can do?...

What the interviewer is asking/looking for: The interviewer hopes you will grab this amount without ever learning he or she was prepared to pay $5,000 to $10,000 more.

Good answer: Repeat the amount offered in a reflective tone, and then be silent—or say "hmmm" and be silent.

Silence seems to unnerve interviewers, who often rush in to fill the vacuum with a higher amount. Try it—it often works like a charm.

Or say you're very close, since the range you were considering was X to Y—with your low end a bit lower than the high end (or fixed amount) the interviewer offered. For example, he or she offers $35,000; counter by saying you're pretty close, since you had a $34,000 to $40,000 range in mind.

Bad answer: You grab the amount offered without negotiation, so they get you at a bargain rate. Or you say no because you want X and he or she said Y—and don't realize there may be "wiggle room" to go up from Y.

Summary

You've learned the importance of timing: how to stall on salary questions, how to wait for the interviewer to throw out the first number, and how prudent silence may buy thousands of dollars in a salary offer. You know to avoid fixed numbers, and stay on your current salary as long as possible. You'll never go into an interview blind again, but be armed with valuable information about how much your qualifications are worth and how to prove you deserve a certain salary.

But you've been interrogated enough.

• Postpone discussing salary until you get a job offer.

• Wait for the interviewer to reveal a salary figure.

• Avoid revealing your past salaries if you can.

• Don't mention fixed numbers, only ranges.

• Research salaries in classified ads, on websites, and by talking to employees and/or trade associations.

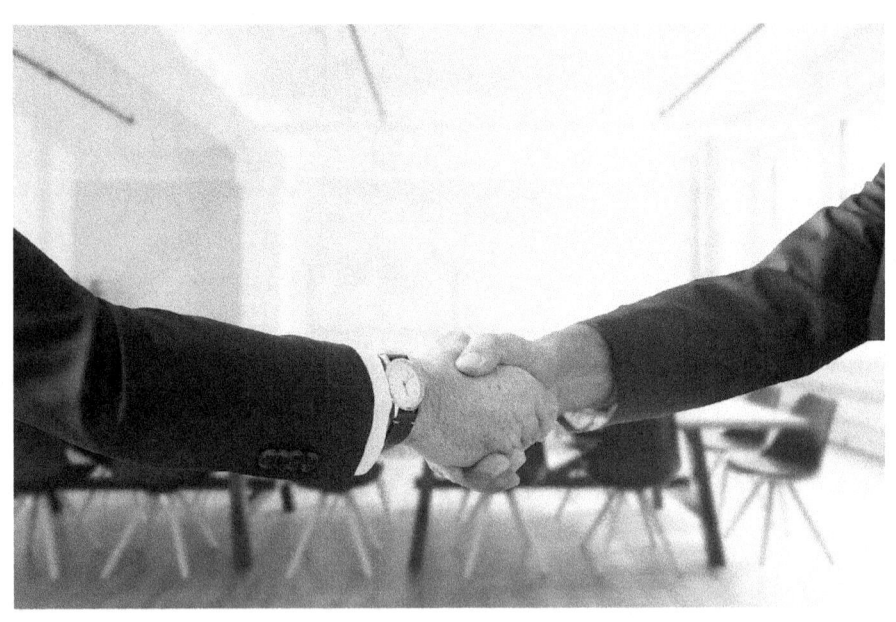

Chapter 13: Saying Thank You

When you are invited to an interview, it is crucial that you know how to say thank you, because this shows gratitude, humility, and a sense of grace toward the interviewer and the HR team. It is likely that HR has looked at many different candidates. They have spent a lot of time reviewing applications and therefore have done a lot of work to weed out candidates and find people who are qualified to do the job. They chose you for a reason, but clearly, it took them some time to sift through all the applications to reach yours. Therefore, you should feel thankful that you got the interview in the first place.

To demonstrate that you are thankful, you should say thank you immediately when you walk into the room and do the interview. This is a step that many people forego and do not remember, but when you do it, you demonstrate a level that is above the average candidate. So, you should say something to the interviewer like the following: *Thank you for inviting me to have this interview. I appreciate the time that you have committed to talk to me about this available position.* You don't have to fluff up your words or try to make it into something fancy. Instead, keep it simple and to the point, because then you can show your gratitude to the interviewer.

In addition to expressing thanks to the interviewer at the beginning, you should also say thank you at the end of the interview. It is important to begin and end with gratitude, because even if you don't get the job or the interview doesn't go well, you can still thank the interviewer for his or her time, because they will likely be seeing a lot of candidates and have to make decisions based on the interview results. It can be an inconvenience for them to take time out of their busy schedule to do these interviews. You must be mindful of the time, money, and investment in these interviews, because it is a costly affair to replace or hire a new person for a job. It is not something that is easy for a workplace to do. At the end of the interview, you should say something like this: *Thank you again for your time and consideration. I appreciated the chance to talk to you about this position. Have a great day*.

The Thank You Note

Another step that goes above and beyond what is expected is writing a thank you note. This is something that the majority of candidates will not do, but it will result in you becoming an outstanding candidate if you do it. Many people forget to say thank you at the end of the interview. Usually, it doesn't guarantee that you can snag a job offer. Don't think automatically that sending a thank you note is going to get you the job, but it is something that helps remind the interviewer of you and your experience with interviewing them. This is especially important when they are considering a handful of candidates and have to distinguish between them in the results. When you have an interview thank you note, then you can set yourself apart from the other candidates and show that you are sincere and really want the job. Express yourself in writing and share your experience of the interview. Here are some tips for writing a thank you note.

Begin with gratitude

The first thing you should say is something such as this: Thank you for taking the time to speak with me about this opportunity. I appreciated the chance to learn about the job and how I could fit into this company.

You should share how much you appreciated the time that the interviewer took to be with you and talk about what your interview experience was like.

Share about how the company aligns with your goals

Next, you should share how the company's values align with your goals for the future. Talk about your skills and relevant experience and how those would help you succeed in this role. Mention the types of job responsibilities you would be expected to carry out and talk about how your experience will help you do everything that you must do. Talk about how the company has values that align with your personal career objectives. This will assist in showing that you are a good fit for the company.

Mention something you were unable to discuss at the interview

Additionally, you should mention something that you were unable to express during the interview, because there was not enough time or you forgot to include it in your answers. This will show that you remembered something important and wanted to bring it to the attention of the interviewer. Then, the interviewer will also know that you are a good fit for the job.

Talk about how you're the best candidate

Finally, you should leave a strong impression in regards to how you are the strongest candidate for this position. Here, you need to reiterate your skills and experience and talk about how those provide you with the best qualifications for this position. Don't shy away from talking about your professional achievements, and highlight the important parts of your career that make you an excellent candidate for this position.

Example of a Thank You Note

Applicant: John Smith

Richard Tate

Assistant Professor and Native English Teacher Coordinator,

_____ University in Japan

17 November 2017

Dear Richard,

Thank you very much for giving me the chance to come to Tokyo to interview with you. I loved my visit to _____University. It felt nice to be there in the natural surrounding with the mountains in the background. I appreciated hearing about the English program at _____, and I feel that the teaching environment is very conducive to developing as a teacher and having the potential to do some research on the side within the education department.

From what we talked about, teaching English conversation within the context of the General English program and other departments would be a task that I am ready to carry out, having had the experience in Spain as a conversational English teacher for two years. I believe my skills and experience will match the requirements of this position. In addition, I want to take on an active role in the campus community while doing outreach with English tutoring one-on-one and participating in extracurricular activities, all to help the students' English language level. I also want to help prepare students for overseas study and assignments with Business English lessons and interview preparation.

What I wanted to emphasize that I didn't feel I was able to articulate at the interview was that I would choose _____ because of its emphasis on educating the whole person and providing a liberal education to all students. Its concept of instilling creativity in the next generation of leaders is something I really wanted to be part of. I want to teach at the _____ University to equip students to be global communicators, and that is why I am an educator. I want to use my experience as a teacher to inform the best research practices and have the chance to share my ideas with other teachers. This is why I hope to work within the College of Education to inform and inspire the new generation of teachers.

Lastly, I wanted to thank you for taking me around campus at the end of the interview. I was not expecting it, and I'm glad that I could become more acquainted with the campus. It was a wonderful way to show the entire circle of the campus.

I'm still in the process of applying to other schools at the moment, but I think that _____ is a top choice for working as an English teacher.

Thank you for your time and consideration. Have a great rest of your week.

Best regards,

John

Conclusion

It is vital that you include a thank you note in your application to the company. Usually, this will be a final impression that you can make on them prior to either getting a job offer or rejection letter. It is crucial that you emphasize your strengths and potential contributions to the company, because that will be what the interviewer is looking for in your application. Highlight your achievements and the mission of the institution where you are applying. Then, talk about how you would be a good fit for the company. Write using persuasive language that will convince your interviewer to hire you. You could be successful in landing the job.

Conclusion

In summary,

• Write an excellent application cover letter. No spelling or grammatical mistakes. Address the email to the person by name. Don't use mobile text language, like "c u soon." People really do! Follow the instructions in the job advertisement if you are responding to a job ad.

• If you are applying for a job where the company has not advertised, keep your cover letter brief.

• Always tell them what you can add to the business, only if you really can. I have had applicants stating that they can do all sorts of things when by their resume I can see that they can do nothing of the sort.

• Be honest

• Be eager, persistent, positive and passionate

• Follow up

• Learn from your mistakes. If you were not hired, ask why and learn from this.

• Arrive on time for your interview

- Be neatly dressed, have a good posture and a firm handshake.

- Be yourself

- Have questions prepared about what you want to ask the company. This is very important

- Most important of all, do your research on the company, go to their website, google them, research the industry, learn, learn, prepare and prepare.

- Go with a list of good questions. Often the questions you ask the interviewer are the most important part of the interview process. After doing good research, you will have a list of good questions. Make sure that they are good and that the information is not freely available on the internet and the company website.

- Make sure that your CV has no mistakes, is short and to the point, no spelling errors, no grammatical errors, that you give the dates of your employment, starting and ending.

- You could prepare a piece of work that will benefit the company to show them the quality of your work and bring it to the interview. Or something that shows the type of work you can do.

• If you are giving references, make sure you have the permission of the person whose name you are giving to use them as a reference and let them know that they might be expecting a call. If someone does not want to give you a reference, then better that they are not on the list. In some countries there is regulation on what a person can and can't say about an ex employee. I was once given someone's name as a reference and when I phoned her, she was not able to give me much of a reference at all.

• Google the founder of the company, or the HR person interviewing you. You will find a huge amount of information on this person and be able to quickly build up a feeling of what type of person they are. This will give you a good indication of the type of person interviewing you. When you meet with them you will then be able to connect with them on a personal level. This is important to do if you can.

• Social media profile. You can be sure many interviewers have done their research on you, so keep certain social media profiles private if you have any photo of wild parties that you would rather they not see!

• Remember that employers and HR department have a problem, they need a new staff member and need to fill it with the right person. You need to make their job easier, hold of your hand, say that you can do the job, want to do the job and will be an asset to their business. Of course all this needs to be true.

• When offered the job, consider the offer carefully and remember you can negotiate what you want. If you want more pay or more leave, ask for it, you never know. My much younger cousin is a great negotiator, she is great at what she does, but has no hesitation in asking for exactly what she wants when offered a new job. She knows her worth and can do an excellent quality of work to justify this. In my younger days, I was so old school, that when I was offered a job, I was very grateful and took it. I had 4 jobs before starting my business.

• Once you start your job, chances are you will be given a trial period, so work like a rock star. Attitude is key, willingness to do the little things that others don't want to do, greet everyone in the morning with a cheerful smile, if your boss enters the office after you, go and find them and say good morning. This is just a basic courtesy. Follow instructions and remember to report back. Often I will ask staff to do something and they might do it, but not send me an email saying it is done. Confirm that you have followed instructions. Communication with colleagues, your boss and customers is always important.

Okay, so in signing off, just in case you missed something . . . remember preparation is key. I cannot overemphasize this enough. Research on the company and the person interviewing you, will give you such confidence in the interview. I sometimes hear people talking about their employers and it just sounds like want, want, want, want more money, want more leave **etc.** How about give, what do I give to you to deserve an increase or more leave? As an employer the happiness of my staff is paramount to me in every way. I want a happy team and will do all I can to motivate, inspire and help my staff grow. I also want to pay them as much as the business can afford and above the industry norm. Employers do make mistakes and one of the worst is employing someone who is wrong for your company in terms of culture, work ethic and ability to do the job. I have made this mistake before more than once. So the hiring of new staff is extremely serious and I am always delighted to hire someone fantastic as my team is. But it really is a problem to find great new staff and many businesses feel this way, it is a long and tedious process, so if you can make it any easier for us, then you will stand out from the crowd of applicants.

I really do hope that this book has been of benefit to you. So in ending, preparation is key, check your cover letter and cv for spelling and grammatical errors, follow up, be keen and just so don't forget, preparation is key.